THE *alpine* GARDEN

THE ROYAL HORTICULTURAL SOCIETY COLLECTION

THE *alpine* GARDEN

CHRISTOPHER GREY-WILSON

CONRAN OCTOPUS

First published in 1994 by Conran Octopus Limited
37 Shelton Street, London WC2H 9HN

Text and original planting schemes
copyright © Christopher Grey-Wilson 1994

Design and layout copyright © Conran Octopus Limited 1994

A catalogue record for this book is available from the
British Library.

ISBN 1 85029 425 9

Project Editor	Jane O'Shea
Project Art Editor	Ann Burnham
Editor	Helen Ridge
Designers	Alistair Plumb
	Lesley Craig
Picture Researcher	Helen Fickling
Editorial Assistant	Caroline Davison
Production	Sonya Sibbons
Illustrators	Lynn Chadwick
	Michael Shoebridge
	Vanessa Luff
	Valerie Price

Typeset by Servis Filmsetting Ltd, England
Printed and bound in Hong Kong

FRONT JACKET Pulsatilla vulgaris.

BACK JACKET *A colourful rock garden in early summer.*

PAGE 1 Papaver alpinum.

PAGE 2 *Aubrietas, saxifrages and early flowering phlox mix with clumps of cowslips and grape hyacinths.*

RIGHT *Matted thymes, rock roses and* Limnanthes douglasii *intermingle on a rock garden.*

CONTENTS

The fascination of alpines   7

Creating a garden for alpines   15

Alpines in the open garden   33

Contained alpines   69

The alpine house   87

Through the seasons   99

Key plants   105

Index   124

Acknowledgments   128

THE FASCINATION OF ALPINES

Some of the smallest, most colourful and most delightful plants grown in gardens come from the high mountain ranges of the world, where they have adapted to a wide variety of different habitats. What is perhaps surprising is the fact that so many of them are very amenable to cultivation and can be grown in our gardens with relative ease.

The delightful, bright yellow alpine pasque flower (Pulsatilla alpina subsp. apiifolia) bursts into bloom on high alpine meadows soon after the snows have melted from the slopes, with more and more flowers appearing as the snow cover recedes. Later, in the summer, the flowers are replaced by attractive, feathery fruit heads.

7

Ramonda myconi, *a distant relative of the african violet, is a native of the Pyrenees where it is found in rock crevices. A surprisingly drought-resistant plant, it is prized by alpine gardeners.*

Dionysia tapetodes, *a cushion-type alpine, forms a dense bun which is smothered in flowers during spring. A shady cliff-dweller from the dry mountains of Iran and Afghanistan, it is suitable only for alpine house cultivation.*

Gentiana depressa *is a classic Himalayan alpine found on the high meadows and screes of Nepal, Sikkim and Bhutan. It is mat-forming with numerous crowded leaf rosettes which closely hug the ground. The outsize trumpet flowers open in late summer.*

Pulsatilla occidentalis, *a tufted alpine, inhabits the high mountain screes and rocky meadows of western North America. The flowers appear above ground the moment the snow melts. The feathery fruit heads are borne on stiff stalks, 30cm (1ft) tall or more, in summer.*

Alpines are among the most beautiful of any group of flowering plants. It is difficult to believe that such small and relatively delicate-looking plants should inhabit such harsh environments in the wild. All the principal mountain ranges in the world have unique associations of alpine plants which, although small, often bear large and bright flowers which attract a great variety of insects, even in such remote and seemingly hostile environments. The examples illustrated on these pages will give a taste of the remarkable variety of alpines: *Ramonda myconi*, a hardy relative of the african violet, inhabits shaded rock crevices in the west and central Pyrenees, but is found nowhere else, coming into flower in the late spring. *Dionysia tapetodes* forms tight, symmetrical cushions studded with flowers in the late spring and early summer: a limestone cliff-dweller, it is found in the high dry mountains of north-western Iran and the Hindu Kush of Afghanistan. On the high mountain meadows and moraines of the central and eastern Himalaya, above 3,300m (10,830ft) altitude, the spectacular gentian, *Gentiana depressa*, comes into bloom at the end of the long summer monsoon. In the mountains of western North America, the exquisite buds of *Pulsatilla occidentalis*, a close relation of the anemones, push through the ground shortly after the winter snows have melted.

It is perhaps the very smallness and neatness of many alpines that most fascinates, coupled with the fact that these small plants can put on such varied displays of bright, pure colour. Alpines are also among the first plants to come into flower in the year and there is scarcely a month when none are in bloom. Moreover, the average garden admirably suits alpines, for a great variety can be easily accommodated in a relatively small space.

It used to be thought that alpines were only for connoisseur gardeners and that expensive glasshouses and elaborate rock gardens like miniature mountain ranges were needed in order to grow them successfully. Now we know this is not so and that, although some certainly do require specialist and carefully controlled growing conditions, many can be grown

with ease in the open garden. Alpines have never been more popular than they are today: visit any good garden centre and you will find a wide selection of different kinds for sale and there are also many specialist nurseries selling a great range of different alpines. In Britain, the Alpine Garden Society and the Scottish Rock Garden Club have grown significantly in numbers in recent years. Their specialist shows in many parts of the country increasingly attract a large and enthusiastic public which has discovered the rewards of alpine gardening.

Alpines in the wild

In order to appreciate the growing conditions that alpines need in the garden, it is useful to look at the ways in which they are to be found growing in the wild. In any major mountain region, such as the Alps, Pyrenees, Rockies or Himalaya, it is possible to observe a surprising diversity of habitats and plants. The transition of habitats will not vary greatly from one range to another, so let us take an imaginary walk up a typical valley in the Alps.

This lush meadow in the French Massif Central, unspoilt by ploughing or herbicides, abounds with poet's narcissi (Narcissus poeticus), marsh orchids (Dactylorhiza maculata) bistorts (Polygonum) and hawk weeds (Hieracium).

Low down in the foothills there is dense, broad-leaved, deciduous woodland with a rich understorey of shrubs and flowering alpines. Here the open meadows are lush and deep and full of coarse flowering plants and grasses which are quite different from the flora of the adjacent woodland. Marshy areas along the riverbanks harbour quite different types of plantlife again and others flourish on the verges of roads and lanes. As you move up the valley, probably following a little stream, the deciduous woodland gradually gives way to conifers, perhaps with the occasional birch copse. The meadows here are less deep but equally lush, with a great variety of colourful alpines in the spring and summer, the first flowers appearing shortly after the snow melts in the early spring. Used principally for hay and fodder,

ABOVE Ranunculus glacialis, *photographed here in the French Alps, inhabits the frost-shattered, rocky meadows and moraines high above the tree line. The often desolate-looking rocky slopes of the higher mountains are home to some of the most beautiful alpine plants.*

RIGHT *These high mountain meadows close to Mount Baker in north-western USA are typical of rich meadows in many regions of the world which all have their own unique plant associations. Here the colourful medley of alpine plants includes* Lilium columbianum, *white valerians and* veratrums.

these meadows are grazed by cattle once the hay has been harvested. The upper limit at which trees will grow, known as the tree line, varies greatly according to latitude: in Norway it may be as low as 600m (1,968ft), while in Nepal it is not unusual to find trees growing at 4,200m (13,780ft). Above the tree line is the true world of the alpine plant, a world of harsh and varied environments to which a great diversity of plants have become adapted. Here are the high alpine meadows, shorter and less lush than lower down, but carpeted with colourful alpines: easy, everyday alpines such as campanulas, primulas, pulsatillas, buttercups, mountain pansies, geraniums and rock roses, as well as those most glorious of all alpine plants, the gentians with their startlingly blue flowers. Clear, cold streams flow down the slopes of these alpine meadows and, in the hollows of rocky outcrops, late-lying snow patches may last well into the summer. Such hollows are often ringed by a halo of dainty alpines – crocuses, primulas and soldanellas in particular – whose brightly coloured, delicate flowers start to appear as the snow patches gradually retreat. The stream margins and snow hollows will reveal other equally delightful plant associations, as will the peaks, cliffs, ridges and screes all around, as well as the moraines if the region has been glaciated.

At the highest altitudes spring arrives late, occasionally as late as July or even early August, the meadows are left behind and the plants become increasingly scattered and are generally small and ground-hugging, nestling in rock crevices or beneath sheltering rocks. Frequently tufted or cushion-forming, they must endure exposure to searing winds, high light intensity and a short growing season, as well as months buried beneath snow. Their bravura show of flowers during the short spring and summer is witness to their astonishingly successful level of adaptation to such rigorous conditions. Many of these high alpines grow in stony or gritty ground or in rock crevices where, although rainfall might be high, drainage is quick, as excess water soon runs away downhill or seeps through the

rock particles. In such exposed places the wind and sun quickly dry the surface of the ground and the plants spend long periods completely dry, their probing roots seeking moisture from within the rocks.

Alpine plants can therefore be divided into a number of groups according to their natural habitat: high meadow alpines, moisture-loving alpines, scree alpines and high rock alpines. To these must be added small plants found below the tree line but which are suitable for the alpine garden, such as small woodlanders and hardy coastal species. Although technically not alpines at all, many of these true rock plants are ideal for the rock or scree garden. Because their natural growing conditions have much in common with those of true alpines – that is, they grow in open, light situations, often in very well-drained soil and among rocks, away from the fierce competition of trees, shrubs and coarse plants – they will happily grow in alpine gardens. Thus, although in the true botanical sense alpines are any plants that grow above the tree line in mountain regions of the world, in gardening terms the category of 'alpines' embraces a far wider range of plants to include any small hardy plants, whether from sea level or from high mountain peaks, as well as a colourful array of dwarf bulbs.

ABOVE *Rocky slopes close to the sea harbour rock plants in a variety of different colours. In the Greek Peloponnese, a rash of spring colour gives way in summer to a brown and desiccated landscape. Here, trefoils, malcolmias and anthemis compete for a roothold in rocky pockets.*

ABOVE *The author in the alpine meadows of the Cascades, north-western USA.*

Alpines in the garden

Alpines can be grown in a number of ways in the garden, provided a few basic guidelines are followed. Rock gardens and scree gardens, though time-consuming to create, will provide numerous niches for a great range of different types of alpine; however, they are not always practical in very small gardens where space is at a premium and they are by no means a prerequisite for growing alpines successfully. Alpines will grow extremely well in raised beds and are ideal for troughs, sinks and other containers, which can make interesting features for patios, courtyards and terraces: it is surprising just how many of these delightful small plants can be housed in a sink measuring say 90 × 45cm (3 × 1½ft). As with all forms of gardening, some initial effort is required to prepare suitable sites for alpines in the open garden. This effort is amply rewarded by the pleasure of watching them flourish

and there can be immense satisfaction in preparing the right sort of sites, choosing and planting suitable subjects and watching them slowly mature into an attractive and lasting display.

Many alpines are straight species or selections taken from the wild: only a few of these lovely little plants have been adulterated by the endless hybridization that affects other plant groups. A large number thus appear in our gardens just as they would be seen in nature, although over the years interesting variations in colour and form have been selected out to increase the range available. Browsing through alpine plant catalogues can provide hours of pleasure on a cold winter's evening; a good catalogue will give details of height, colour, growing conditions and country of origin of alpines from all corners of the world, as well as indicating whether or not the plant is likely to succeed in the open garden.

Raising plants from seed can add another extremely rewarding dimension to alpine gardening:

Many high alpines are discrete plants preferring space and uncrowded sites. On lower slopes, different species compete and intermingle in the deeper and richer soils, something often difficult to achieve satisfactorily on the rock garden as one element often smothers another. Here, Saponaria ocymoides *forms a tapestry with white* Gypsophila repens *and the clover* Trifolium pratense *with attractively marked leaves.*

there is nothing more satisfying than sowing a pot of seeds, watching the first tiny seed leaves (cotyledons) appear at germination, and then nurturing the plants from tiny seedlings to mature flowering plants – and all this at relatively little cost. In addition, there will be surplus plants to give to friends and to trade with fellow enthusiasts. Many seed catalogues list an assortment of hardy alpine species but it is better to join one of the specialist societies which produce their own extensive seed lists, including many plants that are not available commercially.

A large number of alpine plant enthusiasts have their interest fired initially by attending alpine plant shows, where the benches full of exciting, colourful and varied alpines provide not only a challenge to the newcomer but also the realization that, although some alpines clearly require specialist knowledge and precise cultural requirements, many will succeed quite happily in the open garden. Some gardeners

have been enthused by visits to large public rock gardens or those of expert amateur gardeners. Others become converts on a mountain holiday, where they are seduced by the extraordinary wealth of alpine plants, and return home determined to grow some in their own gardens.

It was in Victorian times that the challenge of alpine gardening first seized the public imagination and interest has grown steadily ever since. The tremendous range of different types of alpine plant now available is a testimony to the dedication and skill of many plant collectors, both professional and amateur, who over the years have introduced yet more of these miniature delights into cultivation. Today, conservation of alpines in the wild is of primary concern, yet through the careful and selective collection of seed, interesting species, hitherto rare or unknown in cultivation, are still being introduced from the wild.

A rocky coastal site is the perfect location for many rock plants provided it is not washed frequently by salt water or sea spray. The spartan conditions of such sites, the lack of coarse, invasive vegetation and the deep rock crevices mimic lush alpine regions and allow these plants to grow uninhibited. Here an association of carpeting rock plants is set off by judicious plantings of dwarf conifers, sun-loving sun roses (Cistus) and lavender (Lavandula).

CREATING A GARDEN FOR ALPINES

Many of the everyday alpines available at garden centres will thrive in the garden without the need for specially prepared beds – aubrieta, arabis, yellow alyssum, some of the thymes, primroses and others are quite happy in the flower border. However, some of the loveliest and most sought-after alpines require more specialist treatment if they are to succeed.

A collection of alpine plants grows in harmony on an established rock garden shown here in early summer. The neat cushion of pink Erodium × variabile *contrasts with the laxer, more informal growth of wall daisy* Erigeron karvinskianus (*syn.* E. mucronatus) *and bright yellow* Hypericum olympicum. *Grey-leaved* Sedum spathulifolium *spreads low between the rocks; attractive year-round, it will flower later in the season.*

15

Starting with alpines

Pink matted phloxes and white Achillea ageratifolia *contrast with the upright growths of cream-flowered* Anemone magellanica *and deep blue, bushy* Lithospermum diffusum (*syn.* Lithodora diffusa) *'Heavenly Blue'. Pink pygmy foxgloves* (Erinus alpinus) *have self-seeded among the rocks.*

Providing the right environment is the key to success with alpines. Specially prepared areas with the right type of soil, correct drainage and exposure will give the plants what they need. It is also important to remember that a great number of alpine plants are very small, even when fully mature, and can be lost in the general garden environment: bringing them together in special areas is therefore not only practical but will also increase your enjoyment of them.

Starting with alpines presents an interesting challenge. The very range and diversity of plants available can prove confusing to the newcomer and it is wise to begin with a small collection of the easier

types, expanding the collection as experience teaches that many are accommodating and generally undemanding plants in the garden. Visit local garden centres as well to become acquainted with the various types of alpine commonly available. Better still, visit a specialist alpine nursery, seek out the proprietor, explain that you are just starting with alpines and ask his or her advice on easy and adaptable subjects. Most owners are only too willing to impart their knowledge and they should also be able to demonstrate alpines growing in different ways – in a rock garden or scree, raised bed, dry wall, sink or trough. From this it should be possible to

Well-bedded rocks form the basis of the rock garden. Rock chippings link the outcrops and provide a pleasing, as well as practical, bed for alpine plants. Here, round stepping stones lead one through the garden, among contrasting mounds of plants. Bright aubrietas are often chosen for larger sites and give carpets of colour early in the year. Many of the alpines in this garden are yet to bloom but the contrast of their shapes, foliage and colour provides interest through the seasons. Towards the back, the spreading and upright shapes of dwarf evergreen conifers give the garden height and emphasize the smaller, discrete shapes of the surrounding alpines.

judge which will be the most practical option for you from the point of view of space and expense. Remember that alpines which do well in one part of the country may not do so well in another; some prefer dry warm conditions and others cool wet ones, so it is wise to visit a nursery close to home to see which species and varieties do well in your area.

The novice alpine gardener is also well advised to join one of the alpine plant societies which, besides holding shows, organize regular meetings, outings to public and private gardens and lectures. These may include practical demonstrations of building a rock garden or raised bed, planting a trough garden or raising alpines from seeds or cuttings, as well as lectures by experts on alpine plants in the wild in various parts of the world. The societies also publish journals and books dealing with all aspects of alpine gardening, as well as producing seed lists which include many rare species and others not available in the trade. All these activities provide a great deal of practical information and expertise that can prove of tremendous encouragement to the newcomer. It says a lot about alpine gardening that so many individuals have developed into expert growers.

Aromatic thymes spread carpets of deep green foliage, accented by other alpines such as small mounds of pink thrift and grey tufts of dwarf fescue grasses. The arching white sprays of encrusted saxifrages push their leaf rosettes into the crevices between adjacent rocks.

Growing conditions

It is disheartening to choose some little alpine gem only to watch its slow demise because you are trying to raise it in the wrong conditions. It is therefore essential to consider a few points before starting.

Soil type

Whereas many alpines, such as *Gentiana* and *Linum*, are quite happy in a limy soil, others require an acid soil and there is a delightful range of charming lime-haters (or acid-lovers) available, including *Celmisia* and *Soldanella*. Soil alkalinity is measured on a pH scale of 1–14. A pH of 7 indicates a neutral soil, while numbers below and above 7 indicate increasingly acid or alkaline soils respectively. You can analyze your soil quite easily with a simple tester available from most garden centres.

It may be that your soil type will need modifying if you are to grow alpines successfully. Acid soils can be changed to be alkaline by adding lime and mixing it in thoroughly until the desired pH is reached – a pH of between 7 and 8 is ideal for many lime-loving alpines. Bear in mind, though, that limy pockets on acid soils will need to be maintained by adding fresh lime every two years as lime is soluble and over a period of time will leach out of the soil. Changing alkaline soils to acid is not possible, however. If acid-loving plants are to be grown and your soil is alkaline, then special beds full of imported, lime-free compost must be constructed.

Aspect

Most alpines thrive best in an open sunny site; do not be put off, however, if you have a partially or wholly shaded garden, for there is still a good range of alpines that can be grown under such conditions.

Rainfall

Watering in one form or another may overcome the difficulties of dry regions, but natural rainfall, which varies enormously from one place to another, is undoubtedly better for alpines and the amount available, especially during the summer months, can greatly influence your selection.

Hardiness

Many alpine plants are perfectly hardy in the open garden, while others are on the borderline of hardiness or require some protection during the winter months. A plant that is hardy in one area, moreover, may not necessarily be so in another. Some knowledge of hardiness can be of great help when selecting plants and it is a good idea to talk to local alpine gardeners and nurserymen about their own experiences. A simple definition of hardiness is not possible, for it is the response of a species not only to

Alpines and herbaceous plants merge to form a carpet of colour backed by white and yellow irises. Genista lydia, a small and shrubby broom that is perfect for the rock garden, forms a mound of bright yellow blooms in early summer and is much loved by bees. The contrasting form of hostas makes an attractive transition between the rock garden and herbaceous border.

temperature but also to a more complex interplay of prevailing factors. Certainly some species will succumb to cold if the temperature falls below −5°C (23°F), say, in damp conditions, but the same species may remain unharmed if the soil is dry at the time. Many alpines survive low temperatures much better in a well-drained soil than in a moist one. At the same time, young plants of certain species may be vulnerable to low temperatures, whereas mature specimens may survive, or it may be the other way round. Again, a plant may die if exposed to biting cold winds in the open garden, but be perfectly happy blanketed below a layer of snow in its distant mountain habitat. Many alpines which have soft woolly leaves are also poorly adapted to moist temperate winters in the open garden, which is why they are often grown in an alpine house where the prevailing conditions can be better monitored. Other factors, such as the time when the plant comes into growth, the rainfall pattern in a particular area, the humidity and aspect will all have an effect on the plant's general hardiness.

Growing alpines

The simplest way to start growing alpines is to try a few small cushion and tufted types (say some saxifrages, dianthus, phlox, drabas and primulas) in a trough, sink or other container, following the instructions for using and filling a trough or sink on pages 78–82. Rock gardens, raised beds, screes and dry walls, all excellent features for growing a wide selection of alpines, are more complicated to construct and relatively more expensive. Experience with a limited range of plants will soon encourage a more adventurous spirit and perhaps the desire to create a larger rock garden with pools and pathways, or to build a raised bed with not only a well-drained area for growing alpines but also wall niches of different aspects to satisfy an even greater range of plants. Seeing plants settle in, thrive and come into bloom is encouragement enough.

related to other, larger cousins growing lower down the mountainside where the conditions are less harsh and exposed. They include dwarf rhododendrons and conifers, diminutive willows, dwarf heaths of various types, small daphnes and a host of other small woody shrubs, some clinging close to the ground and mat-forming in habit. In cultivation many of these species remain dwarf and compact and so are ideal for the alpine garden.

Cushion alpines

One of the most characteristic types of alpine, cushions come in all shapes and sizes, from low mounds to high hummocks, and from those with hard and tight growth to those with a softer and more open character. In some, such as certain dionysias, the solitary flowers are scattered over the

Types of alpine

When it comes to planning and planting alpines in the garden, it is an invaluable asset to be able to recognize the main types and forms of alpines.

Dwarf shrubs

High in the mountains, above the tree line, there are often shrubberies of low bushes or isolated plants dotted across the slopes. These may consist of species

surface of the cushion, while in others, for example many saxifrages, the flowers are borne high above the foliage in spikes or racemes. The cushions may also be formed of hedgehog-like clumps of spiny leaves, as in the acantholimons.

Matted alpines

As well as some dwarf shrubs, there are also many non-shrubby alpines which form mats close to the ground, spreading between the rocks and among other herbs, often flowering in summer. *Pterocephalus perennis* forms soft mats of grey leaves adorned with small, mauvish, scabious-like flowers during the summer, and *Gypsophila repens* forms a mass of interlaced stems with slender paired leaves and sprays of dainty pink or white flowers. Some alpines form mats by creeping and rooting as they spread, while others are anchored by a central root system.

Herbaceous perennials

This is one of the largest groups of alpines with many, very diverse species which are frequently tufted, such as *Gentiana septemfida* and *Geranium cinereum*. They flower year after year but die down to a persistent base at the end of each season. The widely grown *Campanula carpatica*, with its large mid-summer bell flowers in blue, mauve or white

called monocarpic perennials. However, in most rosetted alpines, including the shade-loving ramondas, the rosettes persist and flower for many years.

Annual alpines

Plants which germinate, flower and seed (complete their life cycle) in a single season are relatively rare in the alpine world. *Saxifraga cymbalaria*, a little plant with bright yellow spring flowers which revels in damp shaded places in the rock garden, is a true annual. The charming alpine poppies, which are really perennials, often behave as annuals on the rock garden, flowering and seeding in the first season and dying off during the winter, sometimes to survive for a second or even third season. In any event they often self-sow, which saves the bother of having to resow each season.

BELOW LEFT *Trillium grandiflorum is a North American woodlander well suited to moist, semi-shaded positions. Its unusual-looking, three-petalled flowers appear in the spring soon after the plants start to emerge through the soil.*

belongs here, as do *Incarvillea mairei*, with its exotic pink trumpet blooms and many of the delightful pasque flowers, *Pulsatilla*.

Rosetted alpines

These are alpines which bear one or more rosettes of leaves that slowly enlarge with time. The bristly rosettes of *Meconopsis horridula*, with its sumptuous blue poppy flowers, take one or several years to reach flowering size, then seed and die. Such plants are

Bulbs

The dwarfer types of bulbs, such as crocuses, snowdrops, the smaller fritillarias, tulips and irises make excellent rock garden 'alpines', appearing in the late winter and early spring to give a welcome burst of colour at a dull time of year, and dying away by early to mid-summer. It is wise to remember where they are on the rock garden, in order to avoid chopping them in half during vigorous weeding sessions or when planting fresh alpines.

ABOVE *Bellflowers, often in blue or violet, are gems of late spring and summer, their bell-shaped flowers delighting bees and butterflies.* Campanula aucheri *is not very common in gardens but well worth seeking out.*

ABOVE *Troughs and a wide variety of containers suit a great many alpines. This collection of houseleeks* (Sempervivum) *reveals a bright range of colours and sizes to complement a courtyard or patio garden.*

RIGHT *The deep, gritty scree bed gives many alpines the well-drained conditions of their natural habitats. Even a small scree garden can harbour many different types of alpine to provide interest for most of the year.*

Types of alpine garden

Alpines can be grown in a number of attractive ways in the garden – in rock and scree gardens, raised beds and dry walls. On a smaller scale, troughs, sinks and other containers provide miniature rock gardens.

The rock garden
Rock gardens can be almost any size and should consist of a backbone of carefully bedded rocks with built-in crevices and pockets for alpine plants. They mimic the outcrops and rocky meadows of the high mountains, bringing to the garden similar conditions of rocky and gritty soil and excellent drainage. Although rather expensive to build and requiring a lot of effort initially, they are long-lasting and provide interest throughout the year and, furthermore, can harbour a great range of exciting plants, including true alpines, small shrubs and conifers, as well as dwarf bulbs.

The scree garden
In nature the rocky detritus of screes and moraines high in the mountains harbours some of the most charming and colourful alpine plants, especially those species that demand perfect drainage; in these conditions the exposed parts of the plants remain relatively dry while their long roots penetrate deep into the detritus in search of moisture and nutrients. The scree garden aims to re-create such conditions within the garden and consists primarily of rock fragments of similar or varying sizes, with little soil in the surface layer. It can form a part of the rock garden itself or remain a separate feature.

Troughs
These are ideal for growing a range of small, choice alpines, as the compost can be varied according to the selection of plants: acid or alkaline, a scree mixture for plants requiring perfect and rapid drainage, or a more moisture-retentive compost for small ferns and other moisture-seeking species. Growing alpines in troughs, sinks and other types of container is perhaps the best method for small garden patios or courtyards.

Raised beds
Yet another way of improving drainage and general conditions for the more specialized alpines is to construct raised areas filled with a gritty compost. Raised beds of stone or brick are attractive features in themselves and have the added advantages of bringing the alpines nearer to eye-level as well as greatly aiding routine maintenance. They are also ideal for disabled people, especially those in wheelchairs.

Dry walls
Generally constructed of stone, dry walls (built without using mortar) can provide a specialized niche for crevice-loving alpines and other plants and

In warm, frost-free regions more tender and colourful alpine plants replace the temperate alpines that dislike too much heat. Here, a medley of colours is provided by an assortment of exotic shrubs, annuals and perennials.

alternatives to peat are widely used, including well-rotted compost or leafmould, friable acid loams and some newer composts, such as coconut fibre (coir).

The alpine lawn

High in the mountains, the meadows are studded with low grasses and sedges, interspersed in spring and summer with a tapestry of alpine jewels in bloom, mostly small and colourful. An alpine lawn is more difficult to achieve and maintain in the garden than any other alpine feature: there are few really good examples to be seen, but when they do succeed they can be breathtaking. The main problem lies in choosing a good balance of small plants which will not become too vigorous and competitive and which will happily intermingle with prostrate plants such as thymes and dwarf grasses. Dwarf bulbs are ideal companions for other plants in the alpine lawn.

The frame

Airy frames can be suitable for housing pots of alpines during the summer months and, perhaps more importantly, for protecting them from the vagaries of the winter weather. Pots can be plunged in special beds so that they do not dry out too quickly, especially during hot dry weather. Alternatively, frames can simply be placed over raised beds, either throughout the year or simply in winter, in order to provide added protection. The bulb frame is a similar idea devoted exclusively to the growing of bulbous plants which are mainly dormant through the summer months, when they need to be kept dry. It is generally impractical to mix bulbs and alpines in such frames, as they require different treatment during the various seasons of the year.

are very effective when used to surround a raised bed or retain a bank of soil. Walls facing in different directions can provide sunny and partial or fully shaded aspects to favour different groups of plants.

The peat bed

There are many beautiful and distinctive alpines which do not require a well-drained, gritty compost but instead prefer a moist, acid or neutral bed rich in organic matter, in sun or part-shade. Many such plants are woodlanders in the wild, rather than plants from the high alpine peaks, and the peat or acid bed provides the ideal conditions for them to flourish. Nowadays more environmentally friendly

The alpine house

The alpine house can be any ordinary glasshouse, but ample ventilation is essential and this usually means incorporating more ventilators into a standard design. Some companies manufacture well-ventilated houses especially for the growing of alpines. Plants are usually grown in pots and plunged into special benches in the alpine house, but they can also be planted out permanently into raised beds at whatever height you choose.

Obtaining plants

BELOW Viola septentrionalis *produces an abundance of charming, veined flowers in the spring. Plants form a spreading mat of green foliage with numerous rooting rhizomes, making propagation simple.*

Garden centres generally have a section devoted to everyday alpine plants, many of which are easy to grow but often highly vigorous, spreading all too quickly and swamping their neighbours. Some very attractive alpines, such as certain flowering onions (*Allium cernuum*, *A. flavum*, *A. moly*), some violas (*Viola cornuta*, *V. odorata*, *V. tricolor*), *Muscari* and *Aquilegia* species and *Corydalis lutea*, for example, are

tempting to purchase some of the more specialized and delightful novelties in the hope that somehow they will succeed, though they never will unless precisely sited and nurtured – in which case much money can be wasted, as some of the rarer alpines can be quite expensive. Nevertheless, once you have gained some experience in growing a range of the easier alpines, you may well be tempted into trying some of the more challenging and rarer sorts if you can give them the right conditions.

ABOVE RIGHT Gentiana ornata *is a precious jewel from Nepal and the eastern Himalaya. This rarity will, if well cared for, respond with an autumnal display of bright trumpet blooms held close to the ground.*

prolific seeders and are generally undesirable in the alpine garden, for obvious reasons. It is best to confine such plants to the ordinary flower border or the wild garden. A growing number of garden centres are now selling a larger range of alpines, including more specialized and less familiar plants which deserve seeking out. For the more desirable and discrete alpines it is well worthwhile going to a specialist alpine nursery. It is, however, all too

Choosing plants

It goes without saying that only healthy plants without any sign of pests or disease should be selected. Weak-looking plants or those with abnormal yellowing growth should be avoided, as should pot-bound specimens, starved of nutrients, which have obviously been hanging around for a year too long. These will have a large number of roots appearing through the drainage hole at the base of the pot and rooting into the bed below; damage to the root system is bound to occur when such plants are removed. Dry plants showing obvious signs of desiccation or wilting are also best avoided, as are plants that have only just been potted up.

Pots full of weeds are also a bad idea, as they may well introduce new and injurious weeds to the garden. In any event, all weeds, however small, should be removed from plants before they are planted out. Remember that, as dormant seeds of nasty weeds may lie on the surface of the soil within the pot, it may be wise to remove and discard the surface layer of compost, as small annual weeds introduced on to the rock garden or scree can be very difficult to eradicate. It is also best to resist the temptation to buy large, well-grown specimens for these will be expensive and are often difficult to establish on the alpine garden.

Check the labels on the plants to make sure that the plant is correctly named (as far as it is possible to ascertain) and the label is clearly written. In some nurseries labels will give more information such as height and spread, flowering time and some cultivation details, all of which is helpful in making a final choice of suitable plants.

Be especially vigilant when purchasing plants after severe winter weather and check that the plants are actually alive and undamaged. If in doubt, ask. Sometimes plants will appear to be perfectly healthy above ground but are in fact dead beneath the compost. Conversely, plants that die down during the autumn and winter may leave no trace above ground and in this case it is wise to ascertain that there is actually a plant in the pot. Most nursery owners will be happy to tip out a pot and make sure that a healthy plant resides beneath the compost.

When you get them home, place the plants in a light and sheltered position and keep them moist until the time comes to plant them out. Unfortunate losses can happen at this time if the plants are not properly attended to, especially if they were formerly in some sort of plunge frame. Plants purchased by post should be examined as soon as they arrive to make sure they are fit and healthy. If they are not, then write to the nursery or supplier and tell them.

Most nurseries are anxious to supply their customers with exactly what they ordered and it is in their interests to keep the customer satisfied. Wrapped plants should be uncovered and planted out as soon as possible: give them a drink of water initially if they seem unduly dry. If it is not possible to plant out immediately because of inclement weather or an unprepared site, pot up plants temporarily and look after them carefully in the interim period.

Columbines (Aquilegia) *and pinks* (Dianthus) *contrast in colour and habit. Columbines are prolific seeders, although excess plants are readily removed by general weeding. Pinks, however, will rarely seed around.*

Routine maintenance

Like all other plants in the garden, alpines need a certain amount of routine care and attention. The main aim of this is to keep the alpines attractive and healthy and to make their surroundings as pleasing to the eye as possible. As the maintenance of alpine lawns and peat beds is more specialized, it is discussed separately on pages 61 and 64.

Winter protection

In temperate climates the greatest danger to alpine plants is undoubtedly winter dampness, even when they are grown in well-drained conditions. Most alpines will quite happily tolerate very cold conditions during the winter, in fact many would lie beneath a protective layer of snow in their natural habitat, but dampness, especially during mild winter weather, can prove fatal to some. It is wrong, though, to think that all alpines need careful nurturing during the winter months, as the majority are perfectly happy left unprotected in the open garden. Others, for instance *Physoplexis comosa*, *Paraquilegia anemonoides* and *Draba longisiliqua*, will generally need protecting from excessive winter wet (see also Protecting alpines in winter, below). A sheet of glass or acrylic supported on bricks or rocks can simply be placed over the plant, but make sure that it is secure enough to withstand strong winds. The glass should slope in one direction so that the water runs off it. Cloches can also be used, as can specially made wires; these grip the glass while the 'legs' of the wire are plunged into the ground for stability. Where groups of alpines need to be covered, then larger shelters such as a cold frame or Dutch light frame should be considered; raised beds can be completely protected by a frame supporting a series of glass lights. Protective shields need to be put in position in late autumn and removed in spring. Care should be taken not to let the plants dry out too much, particularly during unusually dry winters or prolonged windy periods. As cushion plants come into flower in spring they may be attacked by birds; wire netting is useful for providing protection against them or, alternatively, black cotton strung between short canes.

Weeds

Weeds can greatly hinder the growth of alpines by competing for available moisture and nutrients and, more importantly, by encroaching on space that could be occupied by more desirable plants. With their vigorous growth they can also smother the more refined and often less robust alpines. Regular weeding will ensure that this does not happen. It is

Protecting alpines in winter

Cushion-forming and soft, hairy alpines that are hardy to the cold but liable to rot in very rainy weather can be protected with a suitable cover, which keeps the rain off but allows adequate ventilation. The simplest method is to place a sheet of glass or acrylic over the plant, leaning it against one rock and securing it under another (see 1, right). Different types of cloche, such as a glass tent cloche (see 2, right), are also effective but avoid enclosed plastic cloches which promote a humid atmosphere, causing fungal rots.

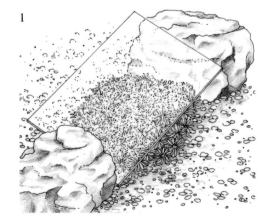

1

2

Netting shields a collection of young alpines from birds which can wreak havoc by pecking and pulling at tufts or cushions. Such damage is especially prevalent in winter and early spring.

undoubtedly a great help to use good sterilized compost and to ensure that the site is absolutely weed-free in the first instance. Despite all precautions, some weeds are bound to invade in the longterm: annual, quick-seeding species such as hairy bittercress (*Cardamine hirsuta*) and pearlwort (*Sagina procumbens*) can be particularly troublesome. Any weeds that do appear should be removed before they have a chance to seed around, otherwise the problem will be greatly compounded.

Annual weeds can be gently teased out by hand. If they have got among choice mat- or cushion-forming alpines, care will be needed to ensure that as little damage as possible is done: hold down the alpine with one hand while pulling up the weed with the other. Sometimes it may be necessary to dig up choice alpines in order to pick out any obstinate pieces of weed.

Perennial weeds are more of a problem. If the infestation is not too serious, then a systemic weedkiller can be applied, preferably in a form that can be simply painted on to the weed's foliage. If a sprayer is used, then great care must be taken not to allow the weedkiller to drift on to the alpines. Two or even three applications of weedkiller may be required to kill a persistent weed. Systemic weedkillers are translocated through the plant and should kill the roots, but some weeds, such as bindweed and sowthistle, have such extensive and invasive roots that they will probably not be killed by a single application of weedkiller. The best time to apply any weedkiller is on a dry, windless day when the weeds are in active growth – late spring to late summer or early autumn.

If perennial weeds are allowed to get out of hand, then you may need to dig up part of the scree or rock garden and eradicate weeds with weedkillers and deep digging. Before doing so, remove any good healthy plants and give them temporary accommodation, cleaning each thoroughly of any obvious weeds. Bear in mind that some alpines (pulsatillas and daphnes for instance) greatly resent disturbance and should not be moved. These will either have to be left *in situ* or replaced; sometimes cuttings of these plants can be taken in advance of removal. Only when the area is completely cleared should the section be replanted.

Some alpines can themselves prove invasive, either by encroaching upon neighbouring plants with very vigorous underground or overground stolons (runners) or else by simply seeding around profusely (see page 24). It is probably better not to plant

27

invasive species in the first instance. Rocks, especially tufa, can quickly become covered in mosses and liverworts which may look very attractive but are liable to smother less vigorous alpines. Scraping with an old knife or spatula is an effective though laborious way of removing them. Moss killer also gives good control and can be bought as a ready-mixed solution in a spray gun. Remember, though, that although the spray may not affect most alpines, it is wisest to keep it off desirable plants to avoid any risk. Always follow the manufacturer's instructions when using any weedkiller.

Top-dressing

Top-dressing serves the dual purpose of keeping down weeds and conserving moisture by preventing the surface of the compost from drying out too quickly. It also prevents compost from splashing around and on to the plants during heavy rain, and keeps the vulnerable 'neck' of cushion alpines dry. Top-dressings of grit or rock chippings will need to be replenished from time to time, as bare patches appear where some of the top-dressing has slipped down the slope or been washed away. Worms can also contribute to the problem by mixing the dressing into the surface compost. If they are not attended to, bare patches may become compacted, especially during heavy rain, in which case they should be eased up with a small trowel or hand fork before a fresh top-dressing is applied. A dressing depth of 2–3cm (¾–1¼in) is ideal.

Top-dressings should harmonize with their surroundings and complement the other rocks. Generally speaking limestone chippings look best with limestock rock, sandstone with sandstone and so forth. Mixing different types of top-dressing is rarely successful, unless it is done with great care. Limestone, or any other calcareous chippings should not be used around acid-loving (lime-hating) plants.

Fresh top-dressing can be applied at any time, but is most likely to be needed in late autumn, when a good layer around choice alpines will certainly help them survive the winter. A further check should be made in spring, before active growth begins.

If the compost in large troughs or on raised beds

has sunk, it can be made up with an extra layer of top-dressing. Whenever top-dressing is applied, care should be taken not to 'drown' the plants: they may survive unscathed, but some will greatly resent being partially buried. Work in fresh top-dressing around each plant, lifting up the edges of plants if possible to push chippings or grit well under the leaves and stems.

Feeding

Alpines, like most plants, respond to regular feeding, especially in long-established areas. The type of fertilizer should be chosen with care – high nitrogen fertilizers which promote vigorous soft green growth are wholly inappropriate for instance. Bonemeal, which is slow-acting, and well-balanced, slow-release fertilizers are ideal, either separately or in combination. Apply them as an overall dressing in spring or early summer, carefully following the manufacturer's instructions, especially as regards the amount to use per square metre. It is best to till the ground around each plant and gently ease in the fertilizer rather than to broadcast it. Fertilizers in powdered or granule form are best kept off the plants themselves as some will certainly cause scorching of the foliage, which may damage choice cushion alpines irreparably. The best method of all is to apply an annual feed with the renewed top-dressing, thus carrying out two operations in one. In old, tired beds, it is a good idea to remove the surface top-dressing, together with the top two or three centimetres of compost, and to apply fresh compost with fertilizer before replenishing the top-dressing of rock-chippings or grit.

New screes and rock gardens made from fresh sterilized compost and incorporating a slow-release fertilizer will not require further feeding for several years. Alpines generally grow away vigorously to begin with, only slowing down as the compost gradually becomes depleted of nutrients. This can usually be detected as a lack of vigour in the plants, often coupled with reduced flowering. On the other hand, many alpines, especially some of the larger cushion types, naturally slow down as they begin to reach maturity.

Pulsatilla alpina
The alpine pasque flower is one of the glories of the Alps and Pyrenees – a harbinger of spring, appearing shortly after the winter snows have melted. The flowers, like open chalices surrounded by a ruff of feathery bracts, can be white or yellow according to the subspecies and are followed by striking, feathery fruit heads, which are borne on tall stalks – a common feature of meadow alpines. The yellow P. alpina subsp. apiifolia *is more often seen in alpine gardens.*

Propagation

Propagating alpines is a fascinating and absorbing pastime. Propagating one's own plants from seed or cuttings is also a cheap way of acquiring additional plants, of replacing old and tired specimens. It is also important in maintaining rare species and cultivars in the garden. In addition, spare plants can be traded for new species with fellow enthusiasts.

Seed

Seed should be fresh and clean and is best sown as soon as possible after harvesting (see Sowing seed, below). Hygiene is essential for success: the compost should be sterilized and the pots clean (plastic pots are ideal). Place a layer of coarse grit in the base of each pot to cover the drainage holes. A standard compost of equal parts seed compost and fine sharp grit or sand will suit most alpines: fill the pots and firm the compost down, water carefully and leave to drain. Sow thinly. Once the seed is sown, remember to label each pot with the name of the plant and the date of sowing. Place the pots in a cool, moist position outdoors such as a sand plunge and remove to a cold frame the moment germination takes place to protect the seedlings. Prick out the seedlings individually when they are large enough to handle – generally when they have developed two true leaves.

Cuttings

Taking cuttings need not involve expensive mist benches and thermostatically controlled propagators. Simple, unheated propagators with a clear plastic hood, which are widely available, can give very good results, as can placing a pot of cuttings in a plastic bag. Take cuttings of vegetative, non-flowering material which should be healthy and strong to

The seed of Viola cornuta *should be collected the moment the fruit capsules begin to split.*

Sowing seed

Prepare the pots as described under Seed, above. Sow the seed evenly and thinly (see 1, right). Cover the surface with a thin layer of compost and add a protective top-dressing of grit (see 2, right). When the seedlings are large enough, prick them out with a spatula, holding them carefully by one of their leaves between thumb and forefinger (see 3, right), and plant into individual pots. These should be filled with a compost and top-dressing similar to that used for sowing. Never allow the seedlings to dry out.

1

2

3

ensure success. A suitable compost for cuttings is a standard soil-based compost with half by volume sharp sand added. Fill pots or trays with this compost and firm it down well. As you remove the cuttings from the plants, store them in plastic bags to stop them from drying out, labelling each type clearly. Cuttings should be 2–6cm (¾–2¼in) long with the leaves carefully trimmed from the lower half. Place them around the edge of the pot or in

Types of cutting

Softwood: the soft growth of actively growing young shoots taken in the spring and early summer, before they ripen.

Semi-ripe: semi-ripened, firm but not woody shoots of the current season, taken in mid- to late summer.

Hardwood: firm, well-ripened, woody shoots of the current year, taken in late summer and autumn. Many evergreen shrubs come into this category.

    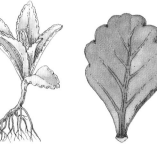  

SOFTWOOD	SEMI-RIPE	HARDWOOD	BASAL AND ROSETTE	IRISHMAN'S	LEAF	ROOT
Anchusa caespitosa	*Cassiope*	*Dryas octopetala*	*Androsace*	*Achillea* species	*Haberlea*	*Carduncellus*
Aubrieta	*Clematis*	Dwarf conifers	*Armeria*	*Arenaria montana*	*Lewisia*	*rhaponticoides*
Campanula	*Daphne*	*Salix*	*Draba*	*Gentiana acaulis*	*Primula gracilipes*	*Gentiana lutea*
Dionysia	*Erinacea anthyllis*		*Helichrysum*	*G. verna*	*Ramonda*	*Morisia monanthos*
Draba	*Hebe*		*milfordiae*	*Primula auricula*	*Sedum* (large-leaved)	*Papaver* (perennial types)
Gypsophila repens	*Helianthemum*		*Saxifraga*	*P. marginata*		*Primula*
Phlox	*Lewisia*		*Sempervivum*	*Veronica*		*denticulata*
Viola	*Polygala*			*peduncularis*		*Pulsatilla* species
				Viola cornuta		

These illustrations show the different kinds of cutting that can be taken from alpine plants. The plants listed under each category are just a few of those ideally suited to that particular method of propagation.

rows in trays with about half of their length inserted in the compost, keeping the lowermost leaves just clear of the compost – except for leaf and rosette cuttings. Water with a suitable fungicide and place in a propagator or plastic bag in a light, but not sunny, position.

Any cuttings that subsequently die or develop mould should be removed immediately to avoid contaminating the whole batch. Once the cuttings have rooted, they will need to be potted up individually using standard alpine potting compost (acid for lime-haters). The roots of young cuttings are extremely delicate and careful handling is necessary to ensure that they are not damaged.

Basal and rosette: many alpine plants have only basal shoots or leaf rosettes which can be removed in spring or summer. They often have only a very short length of stem so they need to be trimmed and inserted with extra care.

Irishman's: the shoots of mat-forming plants often root down, so that cuttings can be removed with a few roots formed already. Treated as ordinary cuttings, they will soon make established plants.

Leaf: a few large-leaved, rosette-forming alpines can be propagated from a single leaf taken in summer or autumn. Leaves should be healthy and mature but not old. Insert the bottom quarter of each leaf into the compost at an angle of 45 degrees.

Root: some alpines with thick fleshy roots lend themselves to this type of cutting and can be taken in autumn or early winter. Dig up the parent plant and remove several good healthy roots. Slice them into 4–5cm (1½–2in) lengths and plant these with the thicker end uppermost (that is the end nearest to the leafy part of the plant). Place the cuttings upright in the cutting compost or in pots of sharp sand so that the top lies flush with the surface of the compost.

Division

Almost any alpine that forms a wide fibrous root system, especially the herbaceous types, can be propagated by simple division of the parent plant (see Dividing alpine plants, below). The divided sections can be replanted immediately where they are required. If you are replacing them in the same site, work the soil over and add fresh compost as necessary.

DIVISION
The following plants are best propagated by division.
Achillea ageratifolia
Alchemilla alpina
Antennaria dioica
Campanula carpatica
  C. cochleariifolia
Chiastophyllum
  oppositifolium
Dianthus alpinus
Gentiana acaulis
Leontopodium alpinum
  'Mignon'
Sagina subulata 'Aurea'
Scutellaria orientalis
Viola cornuta

Campanula carpatica *is propagated easily by division, either after flowering or in the spring as growth commences.*

Dividing alpine plants

Clump-forming plants that become too large will need to be lifted at intervals and divided into smaller pieces for replanting. Divide lifted plants into suitable-sized pieces by teasing the clump apart by hand (see 1, right) or by pushing two hand forks into the clump back-to-back and levering them away from one another (see 2, right). Alternatively, slice the plants up carefully with a sharp knife, taking care not to damage the roots unduly.

1

2

ALPINES IN THE OPEN GARDEN

Although the initial planning and labour can be considerable, a well-constructed rock garden or scree, planted with an array of delightful alpines, will become a major feature of interest in the garden as a whole, providing many hours of pleasure. Public rock gardens tend to be very large but more discreet ones lend themselves perfectly to today's small gardens and, in spite of their size, can harbour numerous small alpine jewels.

Large, carefully placed rocks add grandeur to this well-planned alpine garden. Simple planting complements the architecture of the rocks, while running water provides movement in an otherwise static setting. This garden shows a keen sense of design and a perfect balance between rocks and plants – overplanting would have obscured its attractive structure.

Making a rock garden

This beautifully constructed rock garden, which uses some large and very heavy rocks, is undeniably impressive although it would be costly to build. Such a site makes a realistic and natural setting for a great many alpine plants.

A rock garden can be a handsome feature providing a suitable habitat for a great range of small, slow-growing alpines. It should also be considered as part of the overall garden design and, because it can be fitted into any size of garden, it is ideal for the small modern garden where space is at a premium. As they are so small and compact, many alpine plants can be accommodated in a relatively confined area. Yet rock gardens should not be too small and fiddly. Their impact lies in their shape and overall design, as well as in the way they are constructed to provide niches for different types of plant; they should never be simply a mound dotted with even-sized lumps of rock like a currant bun. Care and thought therefore needs to go into their construction. Large rock gardens can afford to incorporate pathways, streams and pools as part of the overall design, while in smaller gardens they may need to fit in with other features, such as the lawn and flower beds.

Choosing a site

For most purposes an open, sunny site is best, though a similar site facing away from the sun can also be very effective, with the advantage of moderating extremes of temperature. Sites that are shaded for most of the day, overhung by leafy trees, or exposed to fierce cold winds or heavy frosts are best avoided. A sloping site is ideal, so that the rocks can be made to look like a natural outcrop breaking through the general contour of the land, while at the same time allowing for free drainage. In many small gardens, however, the challenge is to produce an attractive outcrop on the flat, and one which not only looks good but also provides a wide range of different niches for plants. This obviously needs careful planning from the outset. Before any construction work is started, the site should be carefully dug over and all weeds removed. Perennial weeds such as sow-thistle, horsetail and bindweed can be extremely difficult to eradicate from an established rock garden, as their roots get under the rocks, so a site infested with them will need to be cleared with a systemic weedkiller well in advance of construction. Weeds should be sprayed when in growth, especially in late spring and early summer. It is essential to follow the manufacturer's instructions for the best results and also for reasons of safety. Apply a repeat application if necessary (see also pages 26–8).

Heavy, clay soils can be more or less impervious to the movement of water and may need to be drained by means of simple drains and a soakaway, especially as heavy rocks and trampling during construction are certain to make the soil even more compacted and waterlogged. Draining a site can involve a lot of work and expense and it is essential that it is planned carefully, but proceeding to construct a rock garden without first installing suitable and adequate drainage will certainly cause a great deal of frustration and disappointment.

LEFT *Alpines and woodland plants compete along the edge of a winding path where the fresh, cool, green fronds of ferns and the young leaves of epimediums make a pleasing contrast with the delicate, yellow blooms of a drift of welsh poppies (Meconopsis cambrica).*

RIGHT *Phloxes (Phlox subulata 'Emerald Cushion Blue' and 'Scarlet Flame') harmonize with a simple arrangement of rocks and gravel, providing interest for many weeks during summer.*

Compost for the rock garden

For the majority of alpine plants a gritty, porous compost mixture with some moisture-retentive organic matter is ideal. The many alpine plants which in their natural habitat grow on a mixture of rocky detritus and varying amounts of organic material, or even directly on cliffs or screes, will all require an extremely well-drained soil incorporating sharp sand or coarse grit. Basic garden soil can be used if it is well-drained and friable: light sandy soils are ideal, while heavy clays are wholly unsuitable. Lime-hating alpines will tolerate only acid soils, but most alpines can be grown on neutral or alkaline soils; some will even tolerate both acid and alkaline.

A good standard compost mixture is one part by volume sterilized loam or garden soil, one part

35

fibrous peat or peat substitute (a friable, sieved garden compost will do) and one or two parts coarse grit or sharp sand. Builder's sand is generally unsuitable as it tends to clog and, being frequently of coastal origin, could contain harmful salt which few plants will tolerate. Variations on this standard mixture can be made up to cater for more specialized plants: many cushion-forming androsaces, saxifrages and *Dianthus* species, for instance, prefer an even

isolate acid-lovers in specially constructed raised beds, troughs or sinks, where the compost will not eventually become limy.

Choosing the rocks

While it is easiest and cheapest to use local stone, certain rocks such as granite and types which weather badly, for example, friable oolitic limestones and shales, are generally unsuitable. Granites and other

RIGHT *In this limestone rock garden, white* Convolvulus cneorum, *with its silvery leaves, contrasts with french lavender* (Lavandula stoechas) *while rock roses add bright yellow in early summer.*

grittier, better-drained compost, so add two or three extra parts by volume of coarse grit or fine rock chippings to the basic mixture.

For acid-loving plants the compost should consist of three or four parts by volume of finely sifted, lime-free leafmould, fibrous peat or peat substitute or even composted bark, mixed with one or two parts of sharp sand. If you make acid (lime-free) pockets in an otherwise alkaline rock garden, it is important that they are isolated with a suitable liner with drainage holes to prevent lime from gradually percolating into the pocket. Lime will always travel downwards through the soil, not up, so that if the basic garden soil is alkaline, the best place for acid plant pockets is on the higher parts of the rock garden. If the garden soil is basically alkaline, it is generally easiest to

hard igneous rocks tend to yield rather featureless lumps which do not make an attractive rock garden, while crumbly, soft rock disintegrates far too quickly to be useful. Rocks with attractive features, especially clearly defined strata (the distinctive layers characteristic of many sedimentary rocks), such as hard limestones and sandstones are ideal, particularly because they can also be split fairly easily, if necessary. These better types of rock are not cheap to buy, however. Some garden centres stock suitable supplies of various types of rock but these are usually graded and there are rarely any very large pieces, whereas an assortment of sizes makes construction easier and the general effect more natural. For larger chunks it is better to deal direct with a suitable quarry, or even visit the quarry and select the rocks

ABOVE LEFT *Warm tones of weathered sandstone provide attractive niches for alpines – blue* Felicia amelloides, *silver-grey leaved* Santolina, *yellow* Hypericum olympicum *and bright red mesembryanthemum.*

ABOVE RIGHT *The wall daisy* (Erigeron karvinskianus), *seen here clambering over sandstone rocks, produces a profusion of bloom in summer.*

personally. Special care should be taken to ensure that any rock, especially well-weathered limestone, has not been removed from a conservation area, or from a site of historic importance or natural beauty. The best types of limestone have becoming increasingly scarce in recent years and if you are in any doubt about the source of the limestone offered, ask.

Tufa, a porous and limy rock that is easily drilled, is ideal for growing alpines. It is also very expensive and rather scarce, and is generally only suitable for small areas, especially in sinks and troughs (see page 83). Few would contemplate constructing a whole rock garden from tufa.

Rock is heavy and often difficult to move around, so it is best to have it delivered as close to the construction site as possible. It is also rough, so it is wise to wear gloves when handling it and to protect your feet with stout boots. Always avoid lifting rocks if possible and never take risks: it is all too easy to crush your fingers, damage your back or sustain an internal injury through handling rocks without due care. Use levers and rollers (see Moving large rocks, below) whenever possible. Large pieces (up to 100kg/2cwt in weight) can be moved easily by using a porter's or sack truck with pneumatic tyres which will ride over lawns without causing too much damage. The biggest blocks can be moved into position using a block and tackle, while smaller stones can be moved in a wheelbarrow.

Moving large rocks

Use a stout iron bar or crowbar as a lever for moving large rocks short distances and for adjusting their position on the rock garden. Leverage can be improved by inserting a small stone as a fulcrum (see 1, right). On flat ground, use a system of strong wooden planks and rollers, such as short scaffold poles. Use an iron bar or crowbar as a lever to move the rock forward. Move the last roller to the front as the rock progresses (see 2, right).

1

2
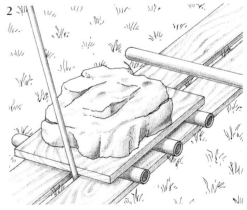

Few gardens can boast a natural outcrop of rocks like the one illustrated here. Clever planting of alpines and herbaceous plants, with the addition of conifers and other shrubs, has made this outcrop an enviable garden feature.

Building a rock outcrop

Dig out a pocket in the soil to provide stability for the largest rock and manoeuvre into position. The rock should tilt backwards and be buried to about one third of its depth (see 1, right). Position the other rocks to the same depth, ensuring all the strata run in the same direction (see 2, right). Once bedded in position, the rocks should look as if they are emerging from the ground like a natural outcrop (see 3, right).

1

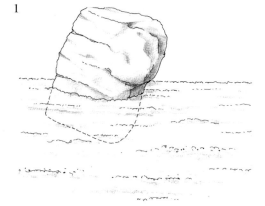

2

Rosette-leaved ramondas (Ramonda myconi), a species found only in the Pyrenees, make ideal plants for rock crevices in the half-shade. Although ramondas look exotic, they are relatively easy to cultivate and remarkably drought-resistant.

Placing the rocks

Rocks need to be bedded correctly if they are to look like a natural rock outcrop. Building a rock garden is not like building a wall: each rock should be placed with care and the relationship between one rock and another carefully considered. Look at the rock closely before positioning it and note any strata, for these must line up in the same direction as they would in a natural rock outcrop. Although in nature strata can tilt in almost any direction, for the purposes of rock garden construction it is most effective if they slope gradually into the soil. This also allows rainwater to seep back among the rocks and plant roots rather than running off on to plants or causing erosion of the soil in front of the rocks, so helping the rocks to bed in properly and producing greater stability.

Start by creating the overall design of the rock outcrop with larger rocks, then fill in with smaller blocks (see Building a rock outcrop, below far left). Blocks can also be laid partly on top of each other, especially on sloping sites, in order to give a tiered effect; they should be set back or stepped for greater stability. As each stone block is placed in position, any gaps between the rocks should be filled with compost which must then be systematically firmed or trodden in to ensure that no air pockets remain and the rocks are properly bedded down. Approximately one third of each rock should be buried in the soil. Tread on them carefully to check for stability – if they wobble, then small rocks may need to be wedged underneath them.

There are no set rules for the shape and design of rock gardens but there is something very pleasing about a well-designed rock garden which has natural-looking valleys, gulleys, screes, ponds and grassy drifts between them. They are also a great deal of fun to plan and build. As construction proceeds, be sure to take an occasional break to check the overall visual effect: it is far easier to make adjustments at this stage rather than wait until the end when every rock is in position. Remember to leave ample pockets for plants between the major rocks. Awkward or unnatural-looking cracks between rocks can easily be filled and masked by judiciously planted small shrubs or dwarf conifers.

3

Filling crevices

The crevices between adjoining blocks are ideal niches for plants (see Planting a crevice, below). These can be incorporated as construction proceeds but it is generally easier to plant up the rest of the rock garden once construction has been completed.

Vertical crevices can pose special problems, however, as soil is easily washed out and the young healthy plants necessary for planting in a crevice will find it difficult to become established. A capping stone or rock above the crevice will help and the crevice itself can be packed with turf fibre or similar material to help prevent erosion. Suitable crevices should be wide enough to accommodate the roots of the plant without squashing them: once properly established the roots will add stability by binding the soil together. Wedging plants into crevices with rock fragments can also be effective, although care must be taken not to damage the roots. It is important to remember that newly planted crevices require careful watering until they have become established, otherwise they will quickly dry out.

FAR LEFT *Crevice plants are among some of the most prized and delightful alpines.* Androsace vandellii *inhabits high crevices in the Pyrenees and Alps in dry, often exposed, places.*

LEFT Primula hirsuta *is also a native of the Pyrenees and Alps, preferring damp crevices and half-shaded positions.*

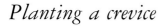

Planting a crevice

Suitable crevices between layers of rock can be planted during construction (see 1, right). Add compost and firm in before positioning the second rock (see 2, right).

When planting a vertical crevice, scoop out some of the compost with a spatula or similar tool, such as an old spoon. Wedge a rock fragment into the crevice immediately below where the plant is to go. Tease the roots apart and ease them into the crevice with the widger, trickling in fresh compost around the roots and firming the plant in (see 3, right).

1 *Tease out the roots of a strong, young plant and position it on a firmed rock with its crown facing outwards.*

2 *The upper rock should be stepped back from the first, inclined at a similar angle, and firmed in well.*

3 *Wedge a second small rock in the crevice above the plant to prevent the compost from being washed away.*

Making a rock garden on a flat site

The flat site presents problems of drainage in many alpine gardens, with the exception of those on light, sandy soils. Drainage can be improved, however, by creating a low mound on which to construct the rock outcrop. The mound can be created by digging out an adjacent area for a rock garden pool (see pages 48–9) and using the excavated soil to build up the site. Do not bury good topsoil: if necessary, move it to one side while you excavate the pool, then put it on top of the poorer subsoil on the mound.

The largest block of rock should be positioned first, tilted and bedded down as described on pages 38–9, to form the leading edge of the rock outcrop. The position of this keystone is critical as all the other rocks should relate to it. On a larger site, there may be more than one keystone but they should still all relate to one another. The other rocks should then be added, behind and sideways from the keystone, with the best rocks used in the most prominent positions and the less attractive and odd-shaped pieces used behind or for infilling. Remember to match the strata lines, as a haphazard arrangement of rocks will never look right and overplanting will not hide poor construction and lack of design.

Alternatively, you can build an island rock garden with an edging of rock blocks to retain the compost and tiers of rocks leading progressively to the middle of the island (see Building an island rock garden, below). It is more practical to use the largest rocks for the lowest tier. The rocks should be bedded and aligned carefully with pockets left for plants. This system is especially effective on heavy, clay soils where it will greatly improve drainage on the rock garden site and, while it produces a rather less natural-looking rock garden than a rock outcrop, it can provide numerous useful pockets for plants.

The island bed, so popular with growers of herbaceous plants, is also an ideal site for a rock garden. Islands can be viewed and approached from all sides and therefore need to be planned with this in mind.

Building an island rock garden

Make a low, rather flat mound with coarse rubble and cover it with a layer of inverted turves to prevent compost being washed down into the rubble. Position the edging of rock blocks and tiers of rocks firmly, infilling underneath and in between them with compost. When all the rocks are in position, fill in around them with more compost so they are buried to about one third of their depth. Spread compost over the surface of the site and around the rocks. Add a layer of rock chippings or grit after planting.

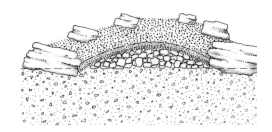

Cross-section of an island rock garden showing the positioning of the rocks.

The same island rock garden viewed from above after it has been planted.

***Globularia
nudicaulis***

The genus Globularia
*contains several superb
little alpines, the smallest
of which are mat-forming
and rock-hugging. This is
one of the larger alpine
species, growing up to
20cm (8in) tall, with
lavender-blue, powderpuff
flowers which appear in
early summer. A tufted
plant, with basal clusters
of deep green, rather
leathery leaves, this alpine
inhabits the rocky slopes
and stony meadows of the
mountains of southern
Europe. It is most useful
planted in the rock
garden, raised bed or
large trough.*

Planting a rock garden

Once the construction work is over, planting can start in earnest. A planting plan, drawn to scale on a piece of graph or squared paper, is a great help and concentrates the mind wonderfully on the overall planting scheme. It need not include every last plant, but the rock outcrops, key shrubs and larger alpines should certainly be indicated. Although they are mostly rather small, alpines still need adequate space and, on the whole, it is difficult to harmonize them in groups as one might in a herbaceous border: cushion alpines, for instance, need a degree of isolation if they are to develop properly. The importance of the surrounding rocks should not be underestimated, however: a good ratio of plants to rocks is essential, for overplanting will spoil the effect and hide all the rocks, while underplanting will look

mean and spartan. The right balance of rocks to plants has to be judged by eye and depends to some extent on the plants chosen and on individual taste – no two rock gardens are ever the same and the flair of the creator is reflected in the structure of the garden and in the juxtaposition of the various plants.

Ideally the rock garden should be planted in time for the plants to settle in and push out new roots before winter sets in: spring and early summer are generally the best planting times but early autumn planting is often successful provided it is not too cold and the soil is moist. Evergreens such as dwarf conifers are best planted in autumn or early spring in all but very mild regions, while most dwarf bulbs should be planted in autumn.

Start with the backbone plants – the small shrubs and conifers that will form a permanent part of the overall structure of the garden. Upright conifers catch the eye and can provide useful highlights on the rock garden, but it is a mistake to overdo them. Dwarf shrubs add interest and can be used as focal points around which the smaller alpines are placed. *Salix* 'Boydii' makes an erect twiggy bush, almost like a gnarled bonsai, with small, oval, greyish leaves; it contrasts attractively with spreading, low growths of sweet-scented *Daphne cneorum* 'Eximia', a must in every alpine garden. *Sorbus reducta* is an unusual dwarf rowan which forms a low thicket, adding colour in the autumn with its bronzed leaves and clusters of pink berries. A neat, rounded shape is provided by *Berberis × stenophylla* 'Corallina Compacta', neat but spiny and covered in late spring with masses of small, orange flowers. A different theme is taken up by the domes of bright yellow *Genista lydia*, whose arching branches are perfect for trailing over the edge of a large rock.

Dig out an ample hole for each plant, set it at the same depth as it was in its pot and firm it in well with the excavated compost. If the plants are potbound, tease out some of the larger roots, otherwise they will have difficulty in penetrating the new soil. Stand back from time to time and take a look to see that the plan is working and the plants are in their right positions; try to envisage what they will look like when fully grown and be careful not to overplant, as this will ruin the whole effect.

FAR LEFT *Succulents will thrive in shallow, dry crevices and are essential for hot and sunny spots. A collection of stonecrops (Sedum) and other succulents provides a surprising range of leaf shapes and colours.*

RIGHT *Where space allows, a drift of alpines can give a very natural look to the rock garden. Here, tufts of thrift (Armeria maritima) fill the crevices and contrast with the bright violet mat of Veronica cinerea, one of the finest speedwells for the rock garden.*

ACID-LOVING
DWARF SHRUBS
These plants need a cool, acid compost to succeed.
Andromeda polifolia
Arctostaphylos uva-ursi
  'Point Reeves'
Cassiope lycopodioides
  C. 'Edinburgh'
  C. 'Muirhead'
Kalmiopsis leachiana
Lithodora diffusa
  'Heavenly Blue'
Phyllodoce caerulea
Polygala chamaebuxus var.
  grandiflora
Rhododendron – dwarf
  species and cultivars
Vaccinium vitis-idaea

RELIABLE DWARF
SHRUBS
These plants will succeed in neutral to calcareous soils.
Berberis × stenophylla
  'Corallina'
Daphne burkwoodii
  'Somerset'
  D. cneorum 'Eximia'
  D. mezereum
  D. retusa
Euryops acraeus
Genista delphinensis
  G. lydia
Hebe pinguifolia 'Pagei'
Potentilla fruticosa
  'Nana Argentea'
Salix 'Boydii'
Sorbus reducta
See pages 122–3 for dwarf
  conifers

Next add the alpines: these present endless possibilities for adventurous planting on the rock garden for they come in so many forms, sizes and colours. Bright mats in many hues of pink, purple and red are provided by the easy-to-grow *Aubrieta deltoidea* cultivars or pink or white *Arabis caucasica*. For a great splash of golden-yellow none is better than *Alyssum saxatile*, although the pale yellow of *A. saxatile* 'Citrina' is perhaps less abrasive on the eyes. Given a nice sunny position, green mats of *Gentiana acaulis*, a plant that is far easier to grow than generally supposed, will dazzle with an unsurpassed show of brilliant blue trumpets. Contrasting shapes can provide interesting arrangements; for instance spiny hummocks of *Acantholimon glumaceum* or *Dianthus erinaceus* both have pink flowers and contrast well with softer shapes such as the grey and white edelweiss *Leontopodium alpinum* 'Mignon' or the grey

and yellow skullcap *Scutellaria alpina*. Saxifrages are an essential element on any rock garden and are many and varied in form and colour. The clusters of small lime-encrusted rosettes of *Saxifraga cochlearis* 'Minor' sprout sprays of white flowers in the late spring. *S.* 'Tumbling Waters' is on a grander scale with handsome leaf rosettes and arching panicles of white, an ideal plant for a rock crevice. In complete contrast are the mats of *S. oppositifolia* with their solitary pink, purple or white flowers which are borne in early spring. Dwarf bulbs can be used with discretion to enliven pockets on the rock garden with colour in spring and autumn (see page 44).

Alpines are best planted when in active growth, especially in the spring and summer. Try positioning them in their pots on top of the soil to make attractive arrangements, combining different growth types to avoid the hummocky look which too many

SPRING-FLOWERING
HARDY ALPINES

Aethionema 'Warley Rose'

Androsace lanuginosa

Aquilegia flabellata 'Nana'

Draba aizoides

   D. rigida

Erinus alpinus

Euphorbia myrsinites

Primula auricula

   P. marginata

Pulsatilla halleri

   P. rubra

Viola cornuta 'Minor'

SUMMER-FLOWERING
HARDY ALPINES

Anemone magellanica

Antennaria dioica
   'Minima'

Armeria juniperifolia

   A. maritima cultivars

Campanula carpatica

   C. cochleariifolia

Carlina acaulis

Chiastophyllum
   oppositifolium

Dianthus alpinus

   D. deltoides

Gentiana septemfida

Geranium dalmaticum

Helianthemum
   nummularium

Origanum rotundifolium

Penstemon newberryi

   P. rupicola

Phlox 'Chattahoochee'

   P. douglasii cultivars

Pterocephalus perennis

Saponaria ocymoides

Saxifraga callosa

   S. grisebachii 'Wisley'
   many kabschia types

Scutellaria orientalis

closely planted cushion alpines can create. If you buy them in flower, it will be easier to contrast the different shapes and avoid harsh colour clashes. When you are ready to plant, first scoop out a suitable-sized hole between the rocks. Remove the plant carefully from its pot and place it in the hole, firming in compost all around. Leave the plant just proud of the compost to allow for a top-dressing of rock chippings (see page 28). If a lot of alpines are being planted out at the same time, the chippings can be added as one operation at the end, after watering. Once you have planted them, water all the plants in well and carry on watering regularly if the weather is dry. The routine maintenance of a rock garden is discussed in the previous chapter on Creating a garden for alpines (see page 26).

Labelling

It is very easy to forget the names of alpines as there are so many to remember, so careful labelling at planting time is invaluable. Labels are invariably ugly and can spoil the look of the rock garden, and white plastic labels, despite their relative cheapness, are especially unsympathetic. However, they can be used inconspicuously by writing the names on them with a permanent marker and then plunging them right down into the compost, close to the plant, so that only the very tips show – this has the added advantage of deterring birds from tossing them all over the garden. When you want to read the label, simply pull it up. Small, grey, aluminium labels, which are far longer-lasting and more discreet, are a better but more expensive alternative.

Dwarf bulbs for the rock garden

Bulbs provide a valuable extra dimension to the alpine garden, enlivening dull corners at unpromising times of year. A large selection is available from garden centres and bulb companies in an almost bewildering range of species and colours. Many, including snowdrops (*Galanthus*), crocuses, *Scilla bifolia* and *Corydalis solida*, flower early in the year, providing interest and colour at a time when there

are relatively few alpines in flower. There are also some, for example *Cyclamen hederifolium* and *C. coum*, that will put on a show of bloom in late autumn or the depths of winter.

Most bulbs, particularly the more specialized dwarf varieties, thrive in well-drained, gritty soils, so standard alpine compost is very much to their liking. Furthermore, the majority relish the open, sunny position of a rock garden and the gritty top-dressing will prevent the delicate blooms from being splashed with mud in wet weather. However, only the smaller, dwarfer bulbs are suitable, except on very large rock gardens, and they must be positioned with care: prolific seeders like many ornamental onions (*Allium*) and grape hyacinths (*Muscari*) should be avoided at all costs. These plants will cast seedlings far and wide (and especially, it seems, into desirable cushion- and mat-forming alpines), and prove practically impossible to eradicate.

Even many dwarf bulbs produce large numbers of untidy leaves after flowering, which not only look unsightly but may also flop on to choice and more delicate alpines. If they are left lying about for long, they can cause dead and unsightly patches on the alpines which are sometimes difficult to remedy. Do not be tempted to remove such leaves too early, however, or the bulb may not make sufficient growth to enable it to flower freely the following season. The answer is to place bulbs with some thought, so that they do not infringe on choice plants. Positioned with care, they can grow happily among low-growing shrubs or mat-forming alpines – small crocuses can look charming growing through mats of thyme, for instance.

Bulbs such as *Narcissus cyclamineus*, *Cyclamen coum* or *C. cilicium*, *Tulipa linifolia* and *Eranthis hyemalis* 'Guinea Gold' look most effective in drifts, where space permits, or in groups; if dotted about at random, they will tend to look lost and lonely. Pockets among the rocks on the rock garden are perfect for bulb clumps and the rather upright growth of many small bulbs can be used to contrast with the more prostrate shapes of the alpines.

Most bulbs can be planted in the early autumn. Choose strong, healthy-looking bulbs and prepare the area by turning the soil over, breaking it down and removing any bits of weed. Add a dressing of bonemeal and plant the bulbs at the depth indicated on the packet – mostly this is the equivalent of three times their own height. Mark where you have planted them, as it can be very annoying to dig into a patch of dormant bulbs by mistake and to chop one or two in half.

Dwarf bulbs are generally unsuitable for any except the largest troughs, as their leaves tend to be too vigorous or untidy. There are exceptions, however, such as the dainty little *Cyclamen intaminatum* with its charming white flowers with faint grey veins and pretty kidney-shaped leaves, *Rhodohypoxis baurii* with its short, hairy, spear-shaped leaves and brilliant summer flowers in all shades of pink, red and white, the tiny yellow *Sternbergia colchiciflora* and *Oxalis adenophylla*, which has neat tufts of grey leaves and relatively large pink or pale magenta flowers.

LEFT Crocus goulimyi *is a popular garden bulb which delights by flowering in the autumn rather than the spring.*

BELOW *Carefully chosen alpines and dwarf bulbs harmonize well on this rock garden. Mounds of yellow* Alyssum saxatile *vie with brilliant blue trumpet gentians* (Gentiana acaulis) *and a dainty, pale yellow narcissus, 'Baby Moon'.*

DWARF BULBS
Allium flavum
   A. thunbergii
Anemone blanda
   A. pavonina
Crocus chrysanthus
   C. goulimyi
   C. medius
   C. pulchellus
Cyclamen repandum
   C. coum
Fritillaria meleagris
   F. michailovskyi
   F. pyrenaica
Galanthus species and
   cultivars
Iris reticulata 'Cantab',
   'Harmony' and 'Joyce'
Narcissus bulbocodium
   N. 'Tête-à-Tête'
   N. triandrus
Pseudomuscari azureum
Scilla mischtschenkoana
Tulipa batalinii 'Bronze
   Charm'
   T. pulchella
   T. tarda

A sunny rock garden

This rock garden, illustrated in late spring to early summer, provides numerous niches for a wide range of alpine perennials, dwarf conifers and shrubs. It is important to achieve a careful balance between rocks and plants so that the appearance of the garden is not marred by over-planting. Many alpines are discrete shapes – buns or cushions, hummocks or upright tufts – and are easily ruined if swamped by more rampant plants. Small shrubs and dwarf conifers give structure to the rock garden. The latter also need growing space and their lower branches can be spoiled if other plants are growing too closely.

1 *Acantholimon glumaceum*: spiny hummocks with grey leaves and spikes of pale pink flowers early to mid-summer.

2 *Aethionema* 'Warley Rose': tufts of slender stems and grey leaves contrast with the upright racemes of deep pink flowers appearing early to late summer.

3 *Alyssum saxatile* 'Citrina': handsome pale yellow version of the common yellow alyssum; flowers mid-spring to mid-summer.

4 *Androsace sarmentosa*: spreading soft grey, hairy mats of leaf rosettes bearing heads of pink flowers in late spring and early summer.

5 *Armeria juniperifolia* (alpine thrift): small, rounded cushion with needle-like leaves; pink flowers appear late spring to mid-summer.

6 *Campanula cochleariifolia* (fairy's thimble): dainty, spreading harebell with blue thimble-flowers late spring to mid-summer.

7 *Chiastophyllum oppositifolium*: succulent green leaves and drooping racemes of yellow flowers in early summer.

8 *Cyclamen coum*: kidney-shaped leaves, often variegated, and small flowers in white, pink or reddish-purple which add interest during winter and early spring.

9 *Daphne cneorum* 'Eximia': spreading, evergreen shrub with delightfully fragrant trusses of deep pink flowers in early summer; greatly resents disturbance of any sort but flourishes if allowed to fill its own space; to 23cm (9in) tall with a spread of 50cm (20in).

10 *Dianthus* 'Bourboule': charming, mat-forming little pink with soft grey leaves and pink flowers in summer.

11 *Dianthus erinaceus*: spiny green hedgehog hummocks with small pink flowers which appear in summer.

12 *Erinus alpinus* (fairy foxglove): small rosettes of deep green, neatly toothed leaves and small flowers in pink, red or white from late spring to mid-summer; will self-seed.

21 *Penstemon newberryi* (mountain pride): leathery leaves on tough stems and cerise-crimson trumpet flowers in mid-summer.

22 *Picea glauca* var. *albertiana* 'Conica': dwarf conifer forming a neat pyramidal or conical shape; 30–150cm (1–5ft) in height.

23 *Picea mariana* 'Nana': very slow-growing, dwarf conifer forming a low bun; grey-blue foliage; to 50cm (20in) eventually.

24 *Pratia pedunculata*, syn. *Lobelia pedunculata*: small-leaved spreading plant with stems rooting down and numerous small mauve-pink flowers in summer and early autumn; of great charm despite being invasive.

25 *Pulsatilla rubra*: ferny leaves and deep red flowers in mid- to late spring, followed by attractive feathery fruits.

26 *Salix lanata* (willow): makes a stiff, rather spreading, deciduous bush with fat yellow catkins in early spring, followed by soft grey foliage; to 90cm (3ft).

27 *Saxifraga* 'Tumbling Waters': large and neat, lime-encrusted leaf rosettes which eventually support arching sprays of white flowers early to mid-summer.

28 *Sempervivum montanum* (mountain houseleek): succulent leaf rosettes and deep purplish-red, starry flowers in mid-summer.

29 *Sisyrinchium bermudiana*: grass-like tufts with violet-blue flowers in early summer.

30 *Sisyrinchium brachypus*, syn. *S. californicum*: fans of grey-green leaves give rise to small yellow flowers borne in succession through the summer.

31 *Sorbus reducta*: true midget rowan; suckering shrub to 50cm (20in) tall; best for its large clusters of pink autumn berries.

32 *Thymus serpyllum* 'Bressingham': mats of deep green leaves with tight clusters of clear pink flowers late spring to mid-summer.

33 *Viola cornuta* 'Minor': dwarf form, ideal for rock gardens; violet to lilac flowers from mid-spring to early autumn; will self-seed.

13 *Euphorbia myrsinites*: stiff, spreading stems; fleshy, grey leaves and, in spring, chrome-yellow bracted flowers; will self-seed.

14 *Euryops acraeus*: sun and shelter suit this small evergreen shrub; whitish-grey foliage and clusters of yellow daisy flowers in late spring and early summer; to 60cm (2ft).

15 *Gentiana acaulis* (trumpet gentian): mats of leathery leaves and large trumpet flowers of rich deep blue in spring.

16 *Iberis sempervirens*: low, flat bush with deep green, leathery leaves and flat-topped clusters of white flowers in spring.

17 *Iris pumila*: dwarf iris with fans of pale green leaves and flowers of purple-blue or yellow in mid-spring; 10–15cm (4–6in).

18 *Juniperus communis* 'Compressa': the upright, grey-green spires of this dwarf conifer give the rock garden scale but it needs to be carefully placed; to 1.5m (5ft).

19 *Linum perenne*: tufted plant with elegant, wand-like stems bearing clear blue flowers with satiny petals in summer.

20 *Oxalis adenophylla*: neatly cut grey leaves which are the perfect foil to the satiny pink flowers which appear mid- to late spring.

Making a rock garden pool

Pools or water channels can provide exciting additional niches for plants in the alpine garden, particularly for those that require plenty of moisture during the growing season. Pools, like rock gardens, are best placed in an open, sunny position, away from large, overhanging trees. On larger sites, especially sloping ones, several pools can be interconnected by a series of channels or waterfalls.

Pools are quickly and easily built using a reinforced plastic or butyl rubber liner. On a flat site, a pool and rock or scree garden can be constructed together, using the soil removed to make the pool for building the raised mound for the adjacent rock garden (see page 41). First, mark out the proposed pool and rock garden boundary with canes or rope and then start to dig (see Constructing a rock garden pool, below right). You should allow for an eventual water depth of about 60cm (2ft) and the sides of the pool should slope a little as this will make it easier to lay the liner. The marginal area of the pool should be shelf-like, about 20–25cm (8–10in) deep and as wide as you wish. Check that the top edge of the hole is level, using a plank and spirit level. Line the hole with a 2–3cm (¾–1¼in) layer of protective material, such as fibreglass loft insulation, old carpet, soft sand or newspapers, to prevent sharp rocks from puncturing the pool liner. You will need to work out the size of the liner, whether it is made of plastic or butyl rubber – it should measure roughly the length of the pool plus twice the depth, by the width of the pool plus twice the depth. Lay the liner evenly across the hole following the manufacturer's instructions. This is best done on a warm day when the liner will be softer and more pliable and will mould better to the cavity of the pool. Once in place and filled with water, trim the edge of the liner back to 15cm (6in) of the pool edge and introduce stone slabs, bricks or turf to the edge of the water to hide the liner from view – slabs or bricks can be mortared into place, ensuring each piece is level. Allow the pool to settle for a few weeks before planting.

Poolside plantings provide a lush 'corner' in the rock garden. Many suitable plants are bold and leafy and, although truly mountain plants, they provide a stark contrast to the small and discrete shapes more typical of alpines. Bog primulas are larger cousins of the smaller rock garden types and marsh orchids, with their spikes of white, pink or purple flowers, are typical of mountain meadows and marshes. Hostas with their handsome foliage make an attractive foil between rocks and pool margins, while the airy tufts of small-flowered siberian and oriental irises (*Iris sibirica* and *I. sanguinea* and their cultivars) add a contrasting form among hostas and lower poolside plants. Care needs to be taken not to overdo the planting as many poolside plants are vigorous spreaders and will soon swamp the area.

Today, most garden centres offer a range of marginal plants that can be selected in bloom, so height and colour can be carefully gauged. On small rock pool sites the margins are best planted with smaller plants, otherwise the neat proportions of the rock garden may be spoilt. Planting can take place at almost any time of year except for mid-winter. As the marginal areas are constantly moist, the plants generally require little watering. However, a vigilant watch should be kept during hot, dry weather to ensure that the water level does not drop too low, otherwise the marginal border will start to dry out.

Primula prolifera is an easy bog primula for marginal areas around pools and channels in the rock garden, relishing rich, moist soils and flowering in early summer. Primulas of this type are best planted in blocks or drifts for the greatest visual impact. With the right growing conditions, they will seed around to provide a steady supply of fresh young plants.

The North American shooting stars, Dodecatheon, are distant relatives of the bog primulas and many species enjoy similar habitats, thriving in damp water margins. The easiest to grow in the rock garden are D. meadia *and* D. pulchellum. *Planted in groups they will bring colour to the garden from the end of spring through to early summer.*

Constructing a rock garden pool

Dig out the pool and marginal area and place the excavated soil where the adjacent rock garden is to be constructed. Place a layer of suitable protective material on the bottom of the hole, then lay the liner – plastic or butyl rubber – across the top (see 1, right). Fill in the area for marginal plants with some of the soil removed during excavation to 5–8cm (2–3in) above the eventual water level. Stable rocks placed along the lip of the marginal shelf will prevent too much soil seeping into the pond (see 2, right).

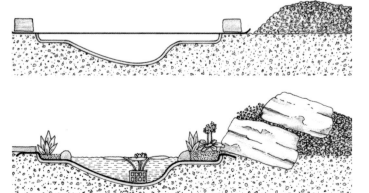

1 *Weigh down the edges of the liner with rocks or bricks to prevent it slipping when it is filled with water.*

2 *Fill the pond slowly with water from a hosepipe, allowing the liner to sink snugly into its final position.*

A rock garden pool

It is best to choose the smaller and less rampant moisture-loving plants for the margins of the rock pool. This pool, shown in early to mid-summer, is planted with bold clumps of bog primulas, their tiers of flowers contrasting well with the upright grassy clumps of *Iris sanguinea*. The marsh marigold (*Caltha palustris* 'Flore Pleno') provides interest early in the year with its bright golden flowers and kidney-shaped leaves. The ferny leaved astilbes add colour in the late summer and hostas, which are available in a great variety of shapes and sizes, relish the moisture of the poolside.

1 *Alchemilla mollis* (lady's mantle): neatly lobed grey-green leaves in large tufts set off the sprays of delightful, tiny yellow flowers, produced in late spring and early summer.

2 *Anthyllis montana*: mat-forming plant with pink or red clover-like flower heads in late spring and early summer.

3 *Aquilegia alpina*: large, clear blue, columbine flowers held above a mound of foliage in early to mid-summer.

4 *Astilbe chinensis* var. *pumila*: low-growing neatly cut leaves and dense fluffy spikes of pink flowers in late summer.

5 *Caltha palustris* 'Flore Pleno': the double-flowered form of the common marsh marigold, though less robust and more spreading; flowers in spring.

6 *Dactylorhiza elata*: handsome orchid with shiny, strap-like leaves and dense spikes of intense purple flowers in early summer; 50–60cm (20–24in).

7 *Genista lydia*: small, deciduous shrub growing to 45–60cm (1½–2ft) with low, arching branches; bright yellow flowers late spring to early summer.

8 *Gunnera magellanica*: creeping plant providing good poolside ground cover; grown for its round, neatly toothed leaves which are often bronze when they first appear.

9 *Hosta sieboldiana*: big clumps of handsome ribbed leaves of a delightful bluish-grey and racemes of pale lilac flowers in early summer.

10 *Hosta sieboldiana* 'Frances Williams': yellow-edged leaves; pale lilac flowers in mid-summer; best in dappled shade.

11 *Iris sanguinea*: graceful, grass-like tufts with small, blue iris flowers in early summer; there are also forms available with purple, violet or white flowers.

12 *Primula prolifera*: a bog primula with stately tiers of clear yellow flowers in summer.

13 *Primula pulverulenta*: a clump-forming bog primula with stiff stems carrying tiers of deep red flowers in early summer.

14 *Primula rosea*: a small species for the pool edge with deep rose-pink flowers in spring; will tolerate some shade.

15 *Saxifraga* 'Tumbling Waters': lime-encrusted leaf rosettes; sprays of distinctive white flowers in early to mid-summer.

16 *Trollius europaeus* 'Canary Bird': bold clumps with striking globe-shaped flowers of pure canary-yellow which are produced in late spring to early summer.

17 *Trollius pumilus*: buttercup-like plant with neatly scalloped leaves and large yellow flowers in late spring.

Creating a scree bed

Screes and moraines are natural elements in the landscape of high mountainous regions and they harbour many delightful alpine plants. Their artificial equivalent in the garden is the scree bed, which can either stand alone as a distinct feature or form an integral part of the rock garden. Its essential characteristics are excellent drainage and fragmented rocks – the type of rock is not critical. When a scree is constructed in conjunction with a rock garden, however, the rock used should be of a similar type or colour; sometimes two rock types can be combined with care – the same rock chippings which top-dress the rock garden could be used for the scree, for instance. The size of the rock fragments can vary greatly, although in general it is easier to plant in less coarse material. A mixture of rock fragments and grit will give the scree a more naturalistic look, in contrast to the carefully bedded rocks and formality of the rock garden.

The same rules of drainage and siting that apply to rock gardens apply equally to screes. A sloping site is ideal, as it promotes the good drainage down a slope that many scree plants like. The area should be marked out carefully with pegs and rope before you start digging (see Making a scree bed, below right). On a flat site the scree is best raised above the ground slightly to assist drainage by including it within a low brick or rock surround – in effect making a low, raised bed. Scree beds should be firmed down well by systematic treading or kneading, watered in generously and allowed to settle before planting is started. As with raised beds, they may subside and need to be topped up with more scree mixture.

Planting a scree

The garden scree is very different from the steep screes and talus slopes of mountain regions, yet the extremely good drainage and random arrangement of rock fragments offer alpine plants essentially similar conditions. Care needs to be taken in choosing plants for screes, as many find it difficult to establish themselves in the coarse, very well-drained aggreg-ate. Good scree plants are those which in nature thrive in a soil that is composed largely of rock fragments. Clearly then not all alpines are suitable for the scree garden, although a surprisingly diverse number are. Spreading and creeping types will work their way between and around the rocks; *Alyssum montanum*, grey-leaved and with masses of bright yellow flowers in the late spring will enliven any scree, as will the softly hairy rosettes and clustered pink flowers of *Androsace sarmentosa* or *A. lanuginosa*.

Campanula cochleariifolia can prove invasive but it is a true delight, a miniature harebell with blue, lilac or white flowers in early summer.

The most exciting scree plants are, however, the discreet little tufts and hummocks of the choicer types which are slow-growing and long-lived. *Gypsophila aretioides* forms green domes of minute leaves, a contrast to the greyer spiny hummocks of *Dianthus erinaceus* or the soft grey cushions of *Erodium reichardii*. Houseleeks (*Sempervivum*) are ideal with their close succulent rosettes in many sizes and colours, providing interest all year, even when they are not in bloom. *Edraianthus graminifolius* bears tufts of slender leaves and violet-blue bellflowers in early summer, in contrast to the spiny hummocks of *Acantholimon glumaceum* with its pink flowers.

Gentiana verna
The delightful spring gentian is aptly named for it is a true herald of spring. Unlike most gentians with their trumpet- or bell-shaped flowers, this species has salver-shaped flowers of a vivid blue which attract both bees and butterflies. It is native to the high alpine meadows of many European mountains, including those of northern England where it is a rare and protected species. Curiously, on the west coast of Ireland it grows at sea level with mountain avens and other alpines.

LEFT Anagallis tenella, *a native of Britain and Europe, grows in marshy areas and, in gardens, requires plenty of moisture. Here, the finest form 'Studland' receives sufficient moisture from the damp scree margin. Small pieces broken off the parent clump will root with ease, or may already have roots attached.*

RIGHT *A patchwork of fragmented rocks and plants epitomizes the garden scree. Equally successful on a gently sloping or flat site, superb drainage is always essential. Although few of the plants on this scree are tall, the contrast of forms and colours provides plenty of interest.*

Making a scree bed

Dig out the marked area to a depth of about 30–40cm (12–16in). Fill in half of the depth with coarse rubble, broken bricks or rock aggregate. Add inverted turves if these have been removed to prepare the site, or a pierced polypropylene sheet. Then add a 15–20cm (6–8in) layer of special scree mixture – 1 part by volume sterilized loam or good garden soil, 3–4 parts coarse grit or rock chippings and 1 part fibrous peat or peat substitute. After planting, top-dress the scree bed with stone chippings, grit or gravel.

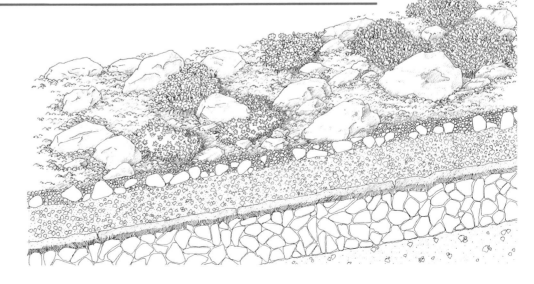

A scree garden

Unlike rock gardens, scree gardens look best as an informal arrangement of rocks of assorted sizes. The most pleasing scree plants are individual tufts or cushions clustered or scattered over the scree. In this scree garden, illustrated in late spring to early summer, persian stone cress (*Aethionema grandiflorum*) and *Campanula portenschlagiana* squeeze into the crevices on the adjoining rock garden, while *Anthemis montana* and *Gypsophila repens* tumble between the rocks at the top of the scree. Spiny hummocks – *Acantholimon glumaceum* and the even spinier broom, *Erinacea anthyllis* – add a contrasting, dense and hedgehog-like form. The spiny theme is also taken up by the pink, *Dianthus erinaceus*, which forms a close dome of sharply pointed leaves.

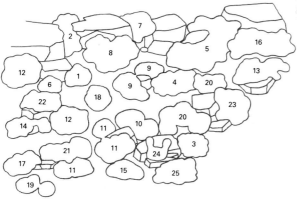

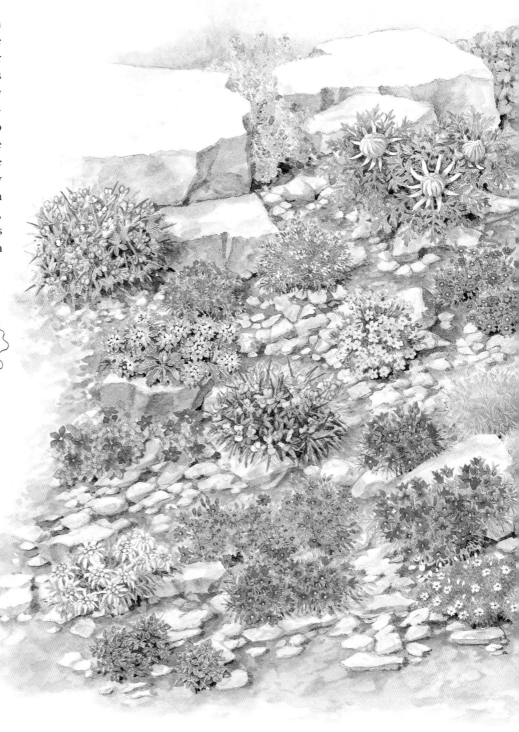

1 *Acantholimon glumaceum*: spikes of pale pink flowers early to mid-summer.

2 *Aethionema grandiflorum*: bluish-green leaves; pink flowers late spring to mid-summer.

3 *Alyssum montanum*: lax, spreading plant with bluish-green leaves and bright yellow flowers in late spring and early summer.

4 *Androsace sempervivoides*: mat-forming rock jasmine; leathery, hairless leaf rosettes; small, pale pink or pinkish-mauve flowers late spring to early summer.

5 *Anthemis montana*: spreading, low hummock of grey dissected leaves and white daisy flowers in spring and early summer.

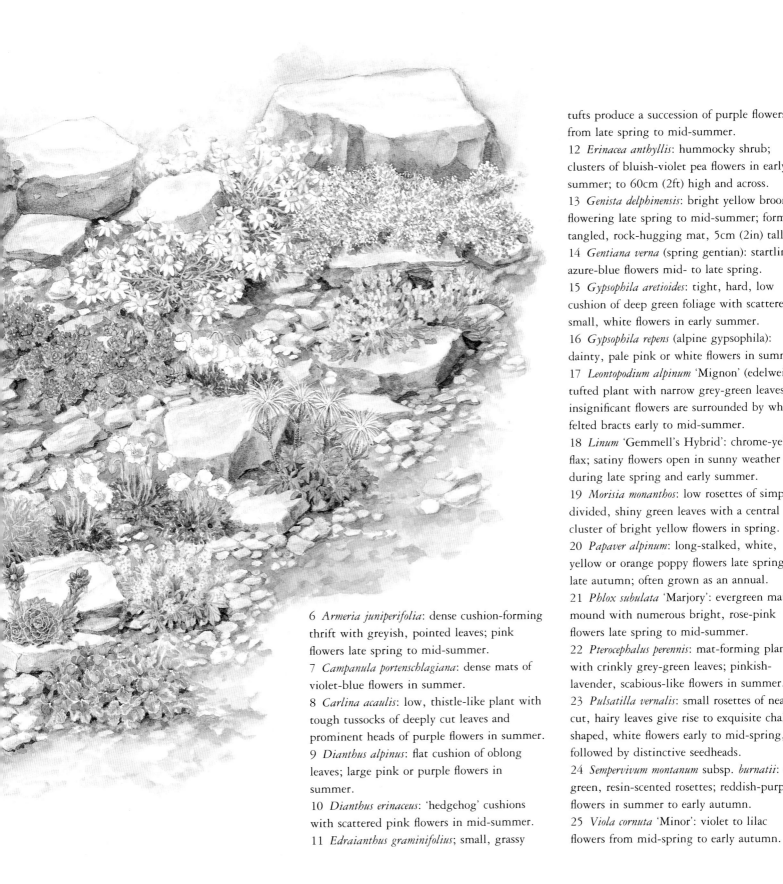

tufts produce a succession of purple flowers from late spring to mid-summer.

12 *Erinacea anthyllis*: hummocky shrub; clusters of bluish-violet pea flowers in early summer; to 60cm (2ft) high and across.

13 *Genista delphinensis*: bright yellow broom flowering late spring to mid-summer; forms a tangled, rock-hugging mat, 5cm (2in) tall.

14 *Gentiana verna* (spring gentian): startling azure-blue flowers mid- to late spring.

15 *Gypsophila aretioides*: tight, hard, low cushion of deep green foliage with scattered, small, white flowers in early summer.

16 *Gypsophila repens* (alpine gypsophila): dainty, pale pink or white flowers in summer.

17 *Leontopodium alpinum* 'Mignon' (edelweiss): tufted plant with narrow grey-green leaves; insignificant flowers are surrounded by white-felted bracts early to mid-summer.

18 *Linum* 'Gemmell's Hybrid': chrome-yellow flax; satiny flowers open in sunny weather during late spring and early summer.

19 *Morisia monanthos*: low rosettes of simply divided, shiny green leaves with a central cluster of bright yellow flowers in spring.

20 *Papaver alpinum*: long-stalked, white, yellow or orange poppy flowers late spring to late autumn; often grown as an annual.

21 *Phlox subulata* 'Marjory': evergreen mat or mound with numerous bright, rose-pink flowers late spring to mid-summer.

22 *Pterocephalus perennis*: mat-forming plant with crinkly grey-green leaves; pinkish-lavender, scabious-like flowers in summer.

23 *Pulsatilla vernalis*: small rosettes of neatly cut, hairy leaves give rise to exquisite chalice-shaped, white flowers early to mid-spring, followed by distinctive seedheads.

24 *Sempervivum montanum* subsp. *burnatii*: dark green, resin-scented rosettes; reddish-purple flowers in summer to early autumn.

25 *Viola cornuta* 'Minor': violet to lilac flowers from mid-spring to early autumn.

6 *Armeria juniperifolia*: dense cushion-forming thrift with greyish, pointed leaves; pink flowers late spring to mid-summer.

7 *Campanula portenschlagiana*: dense mats of violet-blue flowers in summer.

8 *Carlina acaulis*: low, thistle-like plant with tough tussocks of deeply cut leaves and prominent heads of purple flowers in summer.

9 *Dianthus alpinus*: flat cushion of oblong leaves; large pink or purple flowers in summer.

10 *Dianthus erinaceus*: 'hedgehog' cushions with scattered pink flowers in mid-summer.

11 *Edraianthus graminifolius*; small, grassy

SCREE PLANTS

Here is a selection of really good plants for a scree bed.

Acantholimon glumaceum

Aethionema grandiflorum

  A. pulchellum

Alyssum montanum

Androsace lanuginosa

  A. sarmentosa

Armeria juniperifolia

Campanula cochleariifolia

  C. portenschlagiana

Dianthus alpinus

  D. anatolicus

  D. erinaceus

Edraianthus graminifolius

Erinacea anthyllis

Erinus alpinus

Erodium reichardii

Gypsophila aretioides

Leontopodium alpinum

  'Mignon'

Linum arboreum

  L. capitatum

Morisia monanthos

Onosma alborosea

  O. echioides

Papaver alpinum

  P. miyabeanum

Phlox subulata

Pterocephalus perennis

Pulsatilla vernalis

Saxifraga oppositifolia

Sempervivum – any

Silene acaulis

Viola cornuta 'Minor'

  V. jooi

Dwarf shrubs and conifers combine to give structure to this scree bed. Columnar Juniperus communis 'Compressa' and the broader cone shape of Picea glauca var. albertiana 'Conica' provide useful accents. The arched mound of brilliant yellow Genista lydia is a haven for bees for several weeks. The more discrete and colourful alpines – thrift, dainty columbines and white Achillea ageratifolia – form a patchwork of shape and colour, harmonizing with the rock chippings.

The alpine poppies (*Papaver alpinum*) are very delicate with their finely cut foliage and little poppy flowers in yellow, orange, pink or white, yet they are completely hardy and will seed around to give the scree a more natural look. Excess seedlings are readily removed. Similarly, fairy foxglove (*Erinus alpinus*) and alpine toadflax (*Linaria alpina*) are little joys that will multiply quickly by self-seeding to inhabit various nooks on the scree.

Suitable small shrubs can help to lift the scree plantings by providing useful highlights. Spiny hedgehog broom (*Erinacea anthyllis*), for example, has lavender pea-flowers in early summer while the prostrate yellow mats of *Genista delphinensis* are very effective edging a scree where it meets a path.

The roots of healthy pot-grown alpines with a good rootball often have difficulty in penetrating the coarse compost of a scree bed. The best way to overcome this is carefully to knock off most of the compost from around the roots, however unkind this might seem, placing the roots in a hole prepared in the scree, spreading them out in all directions and then infilling with more scree mixture. After planting, top up the surface of the scree with more rock fragments and water the plants in well. Scree plants often develop an extensive root system that will reach out to a distant source of moisture some way down in the scree. Spring is the best season for planting, especially for choicer and rarer plants, though less fussy alpines can also be planted in early autumn. A realistic appearance can be given by a final top-dressing of mixed rock fragments, which needs to be a greater depth than on the rock garden – up to 15cm (6in), but be careful not to 'drown' the plants. It may be better to build up the depth as the plants become established and grow larger. The routine mainten-ance of a scree bed is discussed in the earlier chapter on Creating a garden for alpines (see page 26).

The peat or acid bed

Peat or acid beds provide an acid soil for a wide variety of moisture-loving plants, many of which are woodlanders in the wild, or inhabit mountain moorlands or pockets rich in organic matter in the rocks, while others are true alpines found high above the tree-line. They not only extend the range of alpines that can be grown in the garden but can also be a source of great delight, full of interest for many months of the year.

The conservation of peat is a problem that now concerns us all: as it is so important to the horticultural industry, suitable alternatives such as coconut fibre (coir) compost, utilizing cultivated rather than natural products, have recently appeared on the market. While some of these are excellent for growing pot plants and filling grow-bags, they are more expensive than peat and have not been properly tested as an alternative for growing alpines in the open garden. Until a tried and tested alternative becomes available, peat will continue to be used for peat beds and, I think, the best advice to offer at present is use it but in moderation.

In gardens with naturally acid, well-drained soils, the use of peat can be kept to a minimum: acid-loving alpines can even be grown without using it at all if copious amounts of well-rotted leafmould – which must be neutral or acid in reaction, not alkaline – are dug into the soil. (Leafmould may be acid, neutral or akaline in reaction; if in doubt, test the pH value.) Whichever you use, whether leafmould or peat, you will need to top it up on a regular basis, perhaps every two years, as it slowly decomposes in the soil. Alternatively, you might choose to mix bark chippings, especially pine bark, in with the peat or use them as a top-dressing. Bark chippings are attractive and set off many plants to advantage. A good layer of chippings will also suppress weed growth, especially annual weeds, and act as a mulch to conserve moisture which may be very important during the dry summer months. As well as being both functional and decorative, bark chippings are generally a by-product of plantation forestry and therefore do not deplete the environment.

Siting

The best conditions for a peat bed are dappled shade with some sunshine: a site facing away from the sun which receives filtered light or morning sun is ideal. Avoid full sun and full shade, waterlogged areas or frost pockets; choose instead a position next to the rock garden, on the sunless side of a raised bed or retaining wall, or on the edge of trees or woodland – but beware of vigorous trees with surface roots which will deplete the bed of moisture and nutrients.

Construction

The walls of peat beds have traditionally been built of peat blocks, in the same way as rocks are used in the rock garden, with the blocks being used to enclose small areas and to make pockets and terraces. In most places today, however, peat blocks are both difficult to obtain and expensive, and moreover the concerns of conservation make their use much less

The coolness and moisture of the woodland garden provide a perfect setting for a lush array of shade- and acid-loving plants. Primula japonica *'Postford White' spars with its yellow cousin* P. veris, *the cowslip, and spikes of orchid-like* Veronica gentianoides. *A background of leafy clumps is provided by* Hosta, Epimedium *and indispensable lady's mantle* (Alchemilla mollis).

acceptable. Suitable alternatives for retaining the peat include tree trunks (of species like elm or chestnut which decay very slowly), railway sleepers, low wooden palisades (available in rolls or lengths at many garden centres) and even low brick walls.

On alkaline soils the peat or acid bed should be raised above the surrounding ground and it should never be positioned at the base of a slope, as lime will inevitably wash into the bed and slowly change it from an acid to an alkaline one. Many acid-loving plants such as dwarf rhododendrons and some heathers quickly decline if lime percolates into the peat bed – the first sign is a reduction in vigour and a yellowing of the foliage. A polythene or butyl rubber liner can be put down to isolate the area, but it is important to remember to slope or mound it up in the middle to allow excess moisture to drain away from the bed. A thin layer of sharp sand placed above and below the sheet will prevent sharp stones from puncturing it.

Mark out the area you want to use with a length of rope or hosepipe. The best plan is to build a series of retained terraces, which are easiest to shape into attractive curves and intersections if you use palisades (see Making a terraced peat bed, below) or peat blocks (always remembering the above provisos). Sleepers and tree trunks are more rigid and give a more formal look though this can be tempered to some extent by careful planting, especially if you use

small evergreen shrubs to hide unsightly angles, joins or corners. Whichever material you choose to use, the retaining walls must be properly secured. Trunks and sleepers can be fastened together with giant rivets or staples, inclining them backwards into the bed slightly will ensure further stability. Peat blocks should be moist when used – if necessary, soak them for a day or two beforehand – and well seated in low (5–8cm/2–3in deep) trenches, inclined backwards slightly for stability. Try not to

LEFT Meconopsis horridula, one of the species of Himalayan blue poppy, is exquisite with its transparent 'stained glass' flowers which appear in early summer. The plant is monocarpic, dying once it has flowered and seeded, but in favoured gardens it will seed around freely.

RIGHT The autumn-flowering Gentiana sino-ornata, originating from the high mountains of western China, is essential in any peat garden. Reliable and floriferous, it is always an arresting sight. A large patch will provide enough bloom for the gathering of small posies from time to time. Plants should be lifted and divided every three years to maintain vigour.

Making a terraced peat bed

Mark out the contours of the peat bed with sticks and terrace the slope by digging 75cm (2½ft) wide steps. Dig trenches 7–8cm (2¾–3in) deep, starting with the lowest step, and insert the wooden palisades on end, firming in well and sloping slightly backwards (see 1, right). Fill each terrace with peat or peat substitute to the top of the palisades and tread down lightly (see 2, right). Water thoroughly and allow the compost to settle for a few weeks before planting and top-dressing (see 3, right).

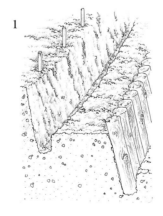

FERNS FOR PEAT BEDS
Adiantum pedatum var.
  aleuticum and var.
  subpumilum
Asplenium trichomanes
Cryptogramma crispa
Onoclea sensibilis
Phyllitis scolopendrium
  P. scolopendrium
  'Crispum'

FLOWERING PLANTS
FOR PEAT BEDS
Astilbe chinensis var.
  pumila
Corydalis cashmeriana
  C. flexuosa
Epimedium davidii
Gentiana sino-ornata
  G. × *stevenagensis*
Glaucidium palmatum
Haberlea rhodopensis
Hacquetia epipactis
Hylomecon japonicum
Jeffersonia dubia
Meconopsis horridula
  M. quintuplinervia
Primula edgeworthii
  P. sieboldii
  P. sonchifolia
  P. whitei
Ramonda myconi
  R. nathaliae
Sanguinaria canadensis
  'Plena'
Soldanella villosa
Uvularia grandiflora

walk on the blocks too often in order to avoid damaging them. If you add a second or third layer of blocks, set them back slightly from the first layer with the blocks overlapping the joints of the lower row, just as you would if building a retaining wall. Sharpened canes or hazel twigs pushed down through the blocks at intervals will bind them together until the plants have become established and add greater stability to the whole bed. Small gaps left between peat blocks or sleepers will allow planting space for crevice plants, such as ramondas and haberleas, and give the area a more mature look.

Infilling

The ideal compost for the peat or acid bed is a mixture of two parts of coarse fibrous peat (fine dark sedge peat is wholly unsuitable) or peat substitute such as acid leafmould, coconut fibre (coir) or well-rotted and sieved garden compost, to two parts of fibrous acid loam, preferably sterilized to prevent weeds from germinating. Any composts with a pH greater than 6.5 will be increasingly alkaline and will certainly not suit acid-loving alpines and certain woodland plants. Fill the bed, terraces and pockets generously, kneading and treading the compost down firmly all over, especially in the corners and along the edges. Water the bed thoroughly and leave it to settle for several weeks before starting to plant. During this time it may be necessary to water the bed to keep it moist; this is particularly important just before planting. If necessary, top the bed up with more compost.

Planting a peat bed

SHRUBS FOR
PEAT BEDS
Andromeda polifolia
  'Compacta'
Cassiope 'Edinburgh'
  C. lycopodioides
  C. 'Muirhead'
  C. selaginoides
Gaultheria procumbens
  G. trichophylla
Kalmia microphylla
Kalmiopsis leachiana
Menziesia ciliicalyx
Pernettya mucronata
  'Bell's Seedling'
Phyllodoce empetriformis
  P. nipponica
Rhododendron - numerous
  small species and
  hybrids; choose only the
  dwarfest
Vaccinium delavayi
  V. nummularia

BULBS AND ORCHIDS
FOR PEAT BEDS
Arisaema ciliatum
  A. jacquemontii
Calanthe tricarinata
Cyclamen coum
Cypripedium calceolus
Dactylorhiza elata
  D. foliosa
Erythronium hendersonii
Fritillaria camschatcensis
Lilium mackliniae
Narcissus bulbocodium
Trillium grandiflorum
  T. grandiflorum 'Flore
  Pleno'
  T. rivale
  T. sessile var. *luteum*
  and 'Rubrum'

The rich dark compost of the peat garden provides a lush environment for the acid- and shade-loving plants that relish the moisture and coolness of such beds. Ferns are an essential element, providing cool greens and softer tones amongst which the more colourful plants can be established to make a tapestry of interest and texture. The various forms of the hardy maidenhair fern (*Adiantum pedatum*) form small clumps with a filigree of delicate fronds. The hart's tongue fern (*Phyllitis scolopendrium*) is in complete

contrast, with its shuttlecocks of elliptical, uncut fronds. The sensitive fern (*Onoclea sensibilis*) is a creeping plant with pale green, deeply lobed fronds which are often attractively flushed with pinkish-brown in the spring when they first appear.

Some of the loveliest small alpine woodlanders make first-rate peat bed subjects. *Jeffersonia dubia* bears its deep pink, rather poppy-like, flowers in spring as the handsomely scalloped foliage unfurls. At the same time appear the white double flowers of the bloodroot (*Sanguinaria canadensis* 'Plena') which also sports bold and handsome foliage. The smaller epimediums such as *Epimedium davidii* with yellow flowers or white-flowered *E. × youngianum* 'Niveum' make mounds of leaves that are flushed with red or bronze when they are young. Rosetted plants such as

ramondas and petiolarid primulas, for example *Primula edgeworthii*, *P. gracilipes* and *P. sonchifolia*, nestle best by a peat block or log and look especially effective planted in a small colony.

A recent and exquisite addition to our gardens is the Chinese *Corydalis flexuosa* with ferny soft foliage and clusters of dripping blue flowers in spring and summer. In contrast are the small tussocks of *Hacquetia epipactis* with neat foliage and handsome yellow-bracted flowers that are attractive the moment they poke through the ground in early spring.

Shade-loving bulbs are another essential element to provide interest and delight in the late winter or spring with some of the smaller lilies adding colour in summer. In spring, try deep pink *Cyclamen repandum* or *Erythronium dens-canis* with its attract-ively mottled leaves. Yellow *Narcissus cyclamineus* has flowers with swept-back petals and will form a small colony in time. The dwarf *Lilium formosanum* var. *pricei* with narrow, pointed foliage has dispropor-tionately large trumpet flowers in white and pink which add a bonus of delicious scent in the summer, or the extraordinary *Arisaema candidissimum* with its pink- and white-striped arum flowers, followed by bold foliage which needs room in which to develop.

Most planting can be done almost any time of the year, especially if you use container-grown plants,

FAR LEFT Cyclamen coum *reveals its small blooms in the middle of winter to cheer the cold days. Easy and adaptable, it is equally at home on the rock garden or in a woodland setting.*

LEFT Trillium sessile *is a native of North America, suited to the peat border or woodland garden. Slow to increase, it should be left undisturbed to build into a stately clump.*

RIGHT *The woodland provides many exciting small shrubs and alpine plants for the peat or acid garden. Various shrubs provide the backbone to this garden, among which other plants – lilies and trilliums in particular – are placed.*

ROUTINE MAINTENANCE

● Water the bed regularly during hot, dry spells.
● Weed regularly, removing perennial weeds with care. Treat any that have become well established with a systemic weedkiller.
● Check regularly for pests: birds and hedgehogs can prove a nuisance, especially in winter and early spring, by rummaging in the top-dressing or by removing the buds of primulas and spring bulbs – protect these with netting. Mice and voles can also cause havoc by burrowing into compost. Set humane traps or acquire a cat.
● Trim back any shrub branches that become too invasive or are diseased or dead – this is best done immediately after flowering for spring- and early summer-flowering species, in the early spring for the others.
● Cut back fronds of deciduous ferns such as *Adiantum pedatum* during the winter.
● Top-dress the bed every year, or every other year, with fresh bark chippings.
● Collect the seeds of desirable plants such as erythroniums and trilliums as they ripen.

but evergreen shrubs are best planted in early autumn, which gives them time to settle in before the onset of winter, or in late winter or early spring. Place all the plants on the bed before you start planting in order to make attractive arrangements of small shrubs and other plants. Avoid any that are known to be invasive, however attractive, especially if they spread underground, for example *Tropaeolum speciosum*, *Eomecon chionanthum*, *Convallaria majalis* and *Matteucia struthiopteris*, as these will quickly infest the bed and be difficult to eradicate; incidentally, these are good garden plants except in the confines of a small or even medium-sized peat bed. Use low evergreen shrubs to mask joins in the walls and insert trailing species or ferns into crevices. Allow plenty of space for plants to develop their full potential, particularly the shrubs. Next, put smaller plants in the sheltered pockets between the shrubs: these niches are ideal for peat bed specialities such as *Jeffersonia dubia* and *Glaucidium palmatum*, which has handsome leaves and large poppy-like flowers.

Firm all the plants in well and make sure that they are adequately watered. All the plants, especially the shrubs and ferns, should be watched carefully for the first few months and watered at regular intervals until they have clearly settled in and new growth is apparent, otherwise they can easily become desiccated during dry spells at this stage.

Finally, the peat or acid bed can be top-dressed with a 2–3cm (¾–1¼in) layer of bark chippings, which serve the dual function of looking attractive and providing a useful, moisture-retentive mulch.

A peat bed

Lush coolness and dappled shade are the essence of the peat garden. Larger plants, especially rhododendrons and lilies, as illustrated here in late spring, provide an attractive backdrop. In the front, a range of smaller subjects, such as small rhododendrons, cassiopes and vacciniums, provide focal points.

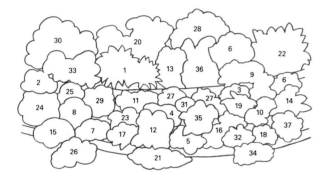

1 *Adiantum pedatum* (maidenhair fern): semi-evergreen fern forming slow-creeping, dissected tufts; bright green fronds on glossy black stalks; 30–45cm (1–1½ft).

2 *Adiantum pedatum* var. *subpumilum*: dwarf version of the above with more congested fronds; 10–15cm (4–6in).

3 *Anemone nemorosa* (common wood anemone): white, pink, purple or blue flowers in spring, followed by a green carpet of foliage.

4 *Anemone ranunculoides* 'Flore Pleno': double, yellow spring flowers followed by a green carpet of foliage.

5 *Asarum europaeum*: spreading carpet of glossy green, kidney-shaped leaves; insignificant flowers.

6 *Betula nana*: small, slow-growing, deciduous, twiggy shrub; neatly scalloped leaves and tiny, yellow catkins in spring; 30–45cm (1–1½ft).

7 *Cassiope* 'Edinburgh': evergreen, dwarf shrub to 20cm (8in) with white bell flowers in spring.

8 *Celmisia coriacea*: large grey rosettes of sword-shaped leaves and big white daisy flowers in early to mid-summer.

9 *Corydalis flexuosa*: dissected grey-green leaves; profusion of exquisite, china-blue flowers mid-spring to summer.

10 *Cyclamen coum*: pale pink to deep magenta-pink flowers in winter and early spring.

11 *Cyclamen purpurascens*: small, deep pink, fragrant flowers in late summer.

12 *Dodecatheon pulchellum* 'Red Wings': tufts of green leaves and long-stalked clusters of pinkish-red flowers with reflexed petals in late spring; 20–30cm (8–12in).

13 *Epipactis gigantea*: vigorous, spreading orchid; slender, ribbed leaves and spikes of green flowers flushed with purple, with a white and chestnut-brown lip in summer; 25–35cm (10–14in).

14 *Erythronium* 'Pagoda': tuberous plant with large, rather fleshy and mottled leaves; pale yellow turkscap flowers mid- to late spring; 25–35cm (10–14in).

15 *Gentiana sino-ornata*: large, royal-blue, trumpet flowers early to mid-autumn.

16 *Hacquetia epipactis*: chrome-yellow bracted flowers from late winter; attractive foliage lasts through the summer.

27 *Primula whitei*: rosette with a dense pin-cushion of blue flowers early to mid-spring; divide regularly.

28 *Rhododendron cinnabarinum*: attractive, upright, evergreen bush; bluish green, oval leaves contrast with the trusses of semi-drooping, waxy flowers of orange or red in late spring; 90cm–3.5m (3–11½ft).

29 *Rhododendron* 'Curlew': small, rounded, somewhat spreading bush with dull green leaves and wide, clear yellow, bell-shaped flowers in spring; 20–30cm (8–12in).

30 *Rhododendron williamsianum*: rounded, evergreen bush with oval leaves attractively bronzed when young; pink, bell-shaped flowers in late spring; 90cm–1.5m (3–5ft).

31 *Saxifraga fortunei*: tufted, semi-evergreen with lax rosettes of fleshy, bronze-green leaves stained with purple beneath; panicles of starry white flowers in autumn; 25–30cm (10–12in).

32 *Shortia soldanelloides*: evergreen, mat-forming; leathery leaves; delicately fringed, deep pink, nodding flowers in late spring.

33 *Trillium grandiflorum* 'Flore Pleno': clump-forming; large, white, camellia-like blooms in mid- to late spring; 30–40cm (12–16in).

34 *Trillium rivale*: small, clump-forming; elegant, three-petalled, white flowers in mid- to late spring; 8–15cm (3–6in).

35 *Trillium sessile* (wake-robin): clump-forming with three large leaves marked with pale green or bronze in the centre of which sits a large, erect, reddish-brown flower in mid- to late spring; 30–40cm (12–16in).

36 *Uvularia grandiflora* (merry bells): erect stems droop at the tips and unfurl yellow, bell-shaped flowers in mid- to late spring; 45–60cm (1½–2ft).

37 *Vaccinium vitis-idaea* 'Minus': low, spreading, evergreen subshrub with shiny leaves and nodding clusters of small, deep pink, bell-shaped flowers in late spring; 5–8cm (2–3in) tall, to 20cm (8in) across.

17 *Iris cristata*: grassy clumps with small, blue, lilac or white flowers in late spring.

18 *Jeffersonia dubia*: purple-blue or white flowers in spring.

19 *Lilium formosanum* var. *pricei*: small lily with a huge, white, scented, trumpet flower in summer; protect from late frosts.

20 *Lilium regale*: elegant, sweetly scented lily; stiff stems clothed in narrow, pointed leaves carry several large, white, trumpet flowers, which are stained pinkish-purple on the exterior, in summer.

21 *Linnaea borealis*: small, shiny leaves; paired, white, bell flowers dangle on elegant stems in early to mid-summer.

22 *Matteucia struthiopteris* (shuttlecock fern, ostrich fern): pale green, rather erect fronds; forms scattered colonies; 75–90cm (2½–3ft).

23 *Narcissus cyclamineus*: bright yellow flowers with reflexed petals in early spring.

24 *Phlox divaricata*: airy clusters of lavender-blue flowers in early summer.

25 *Primula gracilipes*: rosette with a dense pin-cushion of pinkish-purple flowers in early spring; needs to be divided regularly.

26 *Primula vulgaris* subsp. *sibthorpii*: bright green leaf rosettes; pale to bright pink flowers late winter to mid-spring.

The alpine lawn

ROUTINE MAINTENANCE
- Tidy up the lawn in the late autumn, removing old flowering stems and seedheads.
- In the spring trim back any dead growth on thymes and other mat-forming plants and cut back any that are swamping choicer plants.
- Feed established lawns in the spring. A modest feed of long-lasting bonemeal is ideal. Avoid feeding with fish, blood and bone, as it can easily scorch the lawn if used on a sunny day or in dry weather.
- Replace any mat-forming plants that are too old or have become bare in patches. Fork over the area carefully before replanting and incorporate new compost if necessary.
- In summer, keep a watchful eye for ants, which love to build their nests in such lawns, and undermine plants and often kill them. Treat them with a proprietary ant powder, following the manufacturer's instructions.

Colourful meadows are a delightful feature of many alpine regions. Meadows at low altitudes, which are generally cut for hay in midsummer, are vigorous with coarse and widespread meadow herbs. Higher up, close to or above the tree line, the meadows are dwarfer, often strewn with rocks and lush with smaller grasses and alpines which make a delightful patchwork of contrasts. Higher still, the low grass of bluffs and ledges, often studded with little alpines, is kept dwarf by the elements.

Creating such a colourful lawn in the garden is by no means easy, primarily because at low altitudes it is difficult to get the balance of species right, as one or more will tend to become too vigorous and obliterate weaker ones. It is easy to lay an ordinary lawn in a bulb-filled area; mow the bulb leaves after they have died down and plant the lawn with various little wild flowers such as cowslips and ox-eye daisies – though this could scarcely be described as an alpine lawn. A true lawn needs more careful thought. Grass is the chief problem, for few available grasses, if any, suit the concept of the alpine lawn, quickly becoming coarse and unmanageable. What is really required is a grass that does not need mowing and which can be dotted with colourful alpines. The best compromise is to leave out grass all together and replace it with carpeting evergreen plants that provide the basis of the lawn. This effect can be achieved by using cat's foot (*Antennaria dioica*) and even mountain avens (*Dryas octopetala*) as well as mat-forming thymes such as *Thymus serpyllum*. The thymes are ideal and provide a springy 'turf' that is both attractive and aromatic.

Closely planted with other basic lawn plants, such as *Sagina subulata* 'Aurea' and *Chamaemelum nobile*, thymes will form an intricate and close-textured mat which will need little maintenance other than clipping. They can be trodden on occasionally without ill-effect, though they will not stand heavy wear: where a regular route is needed, stone slabs placed at intervals will provide stepping stones.

Alpine lawns can be used as features in their own right or as adjuncts to the rock garden. Constructed with care, they can emphasize the outcrops of the rock garden, making them appear larger and grander. In fact they are a very useful feature for linking rock outcrops, or associating the rock garden with other features such as a scree garden or pool. They can also be very effective if broken up by one or several outcrops of rocks, like high meadows in their alpine haunts. They can be of any size or shape, constructed to equal effect on the flat or on a slope, or they can be made to trail off into the scree or rock garden without an obvious break.

Siting

An open, sunny site away from overhanging trees or the shade cast by buildings is ideal. Avoid a windy position. The area need not be flat; a slope or undulating ground can be very effective, especially if it forms a 'valley' within the rock garden.

Construction

The area needs to be prepared initially with care as the alpine lawn can be a long-term feature in the garden. Remove all weeds, especially perennial ones which will ruin the lawn once established and prove difficult to eradicate. On a free-draining site, dig ample quantities of sharp grit or fine rock chippings into the top 15–20cm (6–8in) of soil. Heavy, poorly drained soils will need drains or a soakaway and greater quantities of grit or rock chippings. Very light sandy soils need no additional material and are especially suitable for thymes. Firm the whole area down. A surface covering of rock chippings gives a pleasing effect but is not essential, as the thyme and other mat-forming plants should eventually cover the ground. If stepping stones are added, they should be set flush with the soil surface.

Planting an alpine lawn

Pot-grown thymes can be planted at almost any time of the year, although spring and early summer are ideal, and should be set 15–20cm (6–8in) apart, leaving gaps if required for other carpeting plants. If

Stepping stones lead across a small alpine lawn which is dominated by scented, mat-forming thymes. The stones create access as well as protecting the plants from being trampled.

FEATURE PLANTS
FOR LAWNS
Armeria maritima and
   cultivars
Campanula barbata
   C. cochleariifolia
Festuca glauca (grass)
Gentiana acaulis
   G. septemfida
Geranium cinereum
   G. sanguineum
   G. var. *subcaulescens*
Pulsatilla halleri
   P. rubra
   P. vulgaris
Sempervivum species and
   cultivars
Sisyrinchium bermudiana
Teucrium pyrenaicum

MAT-FORMING PLANTS
FOR LAWNS
Achillea ageratifolia
Antennaria dioica
Chamaemelum nobile
   'Treneague'
Dryas octopetala
Helianthemum
   nummularium and
   cultivars
Potentilla cuneata
Pratia pedunculata
Pterocephalus perennis
Sagina subulata (syn.
   S. glabra) 'Aurea'
Scutellaria orientalis
Thymus serpyllum 'Albus'
   'Annie Hall'
   'Bressingham'
   'Coccineus'
   'Lanuginosus'
   'Minus'
   'Pink Chintz'
Veronica peduncularis
   V. prostrata
   V. teucrium

you have any large, old, prostrate thymes in the garden these can be lifted and pulled apart to produce numerous partly rooted pieces for the new alpine lawn. The thymes, especially *Thymus serpyllum*, flower in various colours (white, pink, red or mauve) and spread to make a flowery sward greatly enjoyed by bees and butterflies. Other useful carpeting plants, in addition to those mentioned earlier, are *Acaena microphylla* which bears strange spiky red heads in late summer, *Anthyllis montana* with handsome clover-like heads in pink or red, a small yarrow, *Achillea tomentosa*, with moss-like growth and heads of yellow flowers, and *Potentilla aurea*, a typical plant of the high alpine turf, which forms small tufts set with golden blooms in late spring and

early summer. These form the background of the alpine lawn.

Once the basic mat-forming plants are in place, the more discrete species can be planted. These will generally be taller than the mat-forming plants and so able to compete with them with ease. Any that become too vigorous or large can simply be removed and replaced with other more suitable species. Such spot planting should not be overdone, or the lawn effect will be lost. It is also wise to keep to plants that do not exceed 15cm (6in) in height. Experiment with different plants to see which will succeed in your own area. Dwarf bulbs can also be incorporated into the planting scheme; most of those listed on page 45 are suitable.

An alpine lawn

An alpine lawn is a tapestry of colour created by the careful planting of prostrate and low-growing alpines to imitate high alpine meadows. In this lawn, illustrated in mid-summer, an assortment of *Thymus serpyllum* replaces the meadow grass, forming mats of aromatic, deep green foliage which change colour when they come into flower. Contrasting yellow mats are provided by buttercup-like *Potentilla cuneata* and grey-leaved *Scutellaria orientalis*. For a moss-like effect *Sagina subulata* 'Aurea' is unrivalled; although invasive in some parts of the alpine garden, it is ideal on the alpine lawn where it can compete on equal terms with other carpeters. More upright shapes are provided by grass-like tufts of *Sisyrinchium bermudiana*. Grasses themselves need not be excluded – small tufts of fescue grasses, here *Festuca glauca*, mingle well with the flatter mats of the alpine lawn.

1 *Alyssum saxatile* 'Citrina': pale, creamy yellow, billowy flowers mid-spring to early-summer.

2 *Armeria maritima* 'Vindictive': clump-forming thrift with a neat cushion habit and tight, long-stalked clusters of deep pinkish-red flowers late spring to mid-summer.

3 *Chamaemelum nobile* 'Treneague': forms a close, beautifully scented mat of bright green, neatly cut leaves but few flowers; often used for chamomile lawns.

4 *Festuca glauca*: an alpine fescue grass; forms domes of grey-blue leaves to 10cm (4in).

5 *Genista lydia*: non-spiny deciduous shrub with arching green stems covered in bright yellow flowers in late spring to early summer; grows to 45–60cm (1½–2ft).

6 *Gentiana acaulis* (trumpet gentian): makes dense, sun-loving, evergreen mats with brilliant kingfisher-blue, trumpet flowers which are produced in spring.

7 *Helianthemum* 'Wisley Pink': small, spreading subshrub; pale pink flowers are produced in summer.

8 *Helianthemum* 'Wisley Primrose': similar habit but with soft yellow flowers in summer.

9 *Potentilla cuneata*: low-spreading, sometimes invasive, plant with neatly lobed leaves and a succession of yellow flowers all summer.

10 *Pratia pedunculata*, syn. *Lobelia pedunculata*: spreading mats of small leaves and long-stalked mauve-pink flowers through summer.

11 *Pterocephalus perennis*: mats of soft grey leaves support small, scabious-like flowers of pale mauve in summer.

12 *Pulsatilla rubra*: tufts of ferny leaves with rich, deep red flowers in spring, followed by attractive, feathered fruit-heads.

13 *Pulsatilla vulgaris*: similar to *P. rubra* but with violet-blue, purple, pink or white chalice flowers in early spring, followed by attractive, feathery seedheads.

14 *Sagina subulata* 'Aurea': fine spreading, somewhat domed mats of yellow leaves dotted in summer with tiny white flowers.

15 *Saxifraga* 'Tumbling Waters': symmetrical, lime-encrusted leaf rosettes support arching sprays of distinctive white flowers early to mid-summer.

16 *Scutellaria orientalis* (skullcap): forms grey tussocks with bright yellow flowers mid-summer to early autumn.

17 *Sempervivum montanum* (mountain houseleek): clusters of succulent leaf rosettes form tight mounds above which rise stiff clusters of starry, deep pink or red flowers through summer.

18 *Sisyrinchium bermudiana*: grassy tufts produce a succession of violet-blue flowers in early summer.

19 *Thymus serpyllum* 'Albus': deep green mats with white flowers in early summer.

20 *Thymus serpyllum* 'Annie Hall': as for 'Albus' but with soft pink flowers produced in early summer.

21 *Thymus serpyllum* 'Coccineus': as above but with deep crimson flowers in early summer.

CONTAINED ALPINES

Alpine plants can be grown successfully without the expense of a rock garden or scree. Attractively constructed raised beds and dry stone retaining walls provide niches which are perfect for growing many alpines and, where space is at a premium, simple stone troughs in a variety of shapes and sizes offer miniature homes to a range of choice alpine plants, bringing colour and interest to the garden throughout the year.

Retaining walls are used to hold back a bank of soil or to enclose a raised bed. The low, dry wall of this raised bed provides a number of niches for a variety of colourful alpines. Rose-purple Penstemon newberryi caps the wall, accompanied by the drooping pink and white Onosma alborosea. The pink Erinus alpinus has seeded itself randomly into the crevices while the base of the wall is planted with pansies which will bloom for many months.

Alpines in raised beds

Many high alpines grow in extremely well-drained, gritty or stony habitats in the wild (see page 9), and acute drainage is probably the single most important factor in their successful cultivation: hence the popularity of raised beds among alpine gardeners, who use them to extend the range of plants that can be grown in the open garden. Even on a well-constructed rock garden, it is often difficult to get sufficient drainage on a flat site to cater for the more specialized and exciting alpine plants. These need to grow in a well-drained, gritty compost at least 20cm (8in) deep and the easiest way to provide such conditions is to raise the bed off the ground, so that excess water will run out of the bed, leaving the roots of the plants relatively dry. Good drainage should not imply dry conditions during the growing season, however, for most of the plants will require ample moisture: the essential point is that it must never linger around the leafy parts of the plants and must always be able to drain away. The roots of many high alpine plants are long and penetrating and will work their way deep into the compost to seek out the moisture they require – though they will only do so if the compost is of the right texture.

Raised beds are not only functional, but can also be very attractive and, like the rock garden and scree garden, may well form an important part of the overall garden design. Their siting and construction need careful planning and it is also important to bear in mind that they are fairly costly to build, so careful budgeting is advisable. The cost of the retaining wall, for instance, depends very much on the material used in construction, while the compost mixture itself may prove quite expensive, especially for a large bed – it takes a considerable volume of compost to fill a raised bed 2×2m by 30cm ($6\frac{1}{2} \times 6\frac{1}{2}$ft by 1ft) high.

Siting

For the majority of alpines, raised beds are best constructed in an open sunny site, away from overhanging trees or anywhere where water is likely to drip on to them. However, shaded raised beds can be equally successful for woodland plants and alpines that prefer cool conditions (see the planting plans on pages 77 and 80). While some subjects will tolerate full sun, others may need some shade: although many kabschia saxifrages require plenty of light, for instance, they also require some shade during the hot, sunny hours of the day, otherwise they are likely to be scorched.

Whichever aspect you choose, raised beds should, if possible, be positioned so that they can be approached from all directions, which makes maintenance easier. If you decide to build one on a lawn, edge it with bricks or paving stones set just below grass level to make lawn cutting more straightforward. Perhaps one of the best positions for a raised bed is along the edge of a terrace, where it will make a feature to divide the garden.

Size

The larger the bed the greater the cost: on the other hand, small or narrow raised beds can often prove unsatisfactory, as they dry out too quickly and do not provide enough space for plants. At the same time they should not be too wide, so that it is possible to maintain them from the sides without having to clamber all over them to weed and replant: ideally the centre of the bed should be comfortably within arm's reach. Large beds may need to incorporate an irrigation system, for which suitable pipes and inlets must be provided as construction proceeds. A raised bed 2–3m ($6\frac{1}{2}$–10ft) long and 1.5–2.5m (5–8ft) wide is a good starting size. The height can vary: 20–30cm (8–12in) is probably ideal, though some gardeners advocate beds up to 75cm ($2\frac{1}{2}$ft) high. Higher beds have the advantage of allowing a greater number of plants to be grown in crevices in the vertical sides, but they can look a bit odd if the height becomes too great in proportion to length – in the end one has to judge this by eye.

Raised beds have great advantages for disabled gardeners, in particular for those who are confined to a wheelchair and for whom the height and width of the bed are critical.

Oxalis adenophylla

The silky, pink-purple flowers of this South American native are shy and closed during dull weather but open in bright sunshine to reveal delicately veined petals. A jewel of a plant, it should not be confused with the more rampant and weedy types of oxalis.

Materials

Raised beds can be built from a variety of materials. Stone, especially limestone or sandstone, undoubtedly looks best as well as providing an ideal environment for plants. Brick is almost as good and preserved timber, especially old railways sleepers, has the advantage of being relatively inexpensive and lasting for many years. Stone and brick provide better opportunities for leaving spaces in the walls for crevice plants, however. The retaining walls of a raised bed will provide both shady and sunny aspects to suit a wide variety of different plants. Stone walls can be built without mortar and, properly constructed, can be particularly effective for crevice plants. They also allow excess water to drain out sideways through the gaps, as well as downwards.

The stone needs to be chosen with care; the more regular the pieces, the easier it is to build stable walls. Brick walls, on the other hand, will need to be mortared, though it is still possible to leave spaces here and there for crevice plants. Old bricks give a softer, more weathered look than new ones. Your choice of material may ultimately depend on other features in the garden, for stone and brick can look out of place side by side. Whatever the structure, it must be strong and stable enough to retain the compost infill and to withstand being leaned against. Stone and brick walls need to be sunk into the ground to a depth of at least 6cm (2¼in) for stability; vertical brick walls need be only one brick thick and can be supported on a concrete footing 4–6cm (1½–2¼in) deep. Railway sleepers and other wooden blocks may be placed either directly on to levelled ground or slightly sunk into it and can be fastened together with metal pins or braces.

Shape

Raised beds can be of any shape, either regular or irregular, but they should in general harmonize with the rest of the garden and the house. Square, round and rectangular shapes are fairly easy to construct in brick or stone but the shape you choose may well be dictated by the space available and the other design

elements in the garden. Railway sleepers are more restricting, as they really only look their best in designs with straight edges and square corners. Whatever its shape, the raised bed should be an attractive feature in the garden, not simply a giant container for a miscellaneous collection of plants.

Compost

The standard alpine mixture (see page 35) is ideal for raised beds, though more specialized alpines may prefer an even grittier compost, made by increasing the ratio of grit two, three or even four times. This grittier compost is generally preferable in areas of high rainfall (over 100cm/40in per year), while in low rainfall areas (50–60cm/20–24in per year) the standard compost is better. A great advantage of raised beds is that the compost they contain can be different from that in the rest of the garden, so that in alkaline areas, for instance, acid compost can be provided for lime-hating plants. The constituent elements of the compost will probably have to be bought in – though standard garden soil can be used as a basis, providing it is light and friable and free of pernicious perennial weeds – and the amounts required carefully calculated.

This low raised bed retained by blocks of rock provides the ideal environment for those alpines that require extra acute (sharp) drainage. An attractive feature in its own right, the raised bed can be any shape or size and will accommodate a surprising number of plants. Flowering shrubs and dwarf conifers will add height and contrast to the planting.

The formality of these steps and raised beds is enhanced by an informal planting of red rock roses, yellow Alyssum saxatile *'Citrina' and grey-green mounds of pinks. Aubrieta has seeded itself into the cracks of the steps.*

to add strength, and wedge any awkward gaps with smaller rocks as building proceeds. Carry on until you reach the desired height: the top layer – 20–30cm (8–12in) off the ground – should provide a reasonably level surface but this is not critical as plants can be encouraged to tumble over the edge. Plants may either be incorporated in the wall crevices as building proceeds or placed in suitable cracks after completion. The bed can then be prepared for planting (see Preparing a raised bed, below right).

Once the bed is filled with compost, rainfall or irrigation will help the settling process and any subsidence can be corrected by adding another layer of compost. Remember that a planting in a raised bed can last for ten years or more and that over-hasty building and planting, followed inevitably by subsidence, can ruin the whole effect. It is better to wait a few weeks until the bed has stabilized.

If you choose to add rocks at this stage, tufa is ideal, as it can be drilled and planted with relative ease, and hard rocks can be abutted to provide narrow cracks for crevice-loving alpines. Stratified rocks should be aligned just as they would be in the rock garden and all rocks should be bedded in by at least a third and sloped backwards so that water drains down to their base. A few large, well-placed rocks are generally more effective than smaller pieces strewn across the surface and the overall effect should resemble a raised rock garden. If you decide not to

Creating a raised bed

Having chosen the site, ensure that it is level and free of all perennial weeds. Mark it out carefully with canes and rope, allowing space all round for access both during and after construction, and dig out a trench for the foundations of the dry stone wall (see Making a dry stone wall for a raised bed, below). As you build the walls, make sure that each layer of blocks lies across joints in the layer beneath, in order

Making a dry stone wall for a raised bed

Make a shallow trench for the foundations – on heavy, firm ground 5–6cm (2–2¼in) is adequate for a raised bed 20–30cm (8–12in) high but on light, less stable ground a deeper trench, which should be filled with rubble or ballast, is advisable. Construct the base of the wall by using large flat rocks to make a firm platform on which to add further layers (see 1, right). Firm each rock down well, filling the crevices between the rocks with compost (see 2, right). Incorporate plants in the wall crevices as building proceeds (see 3, right).

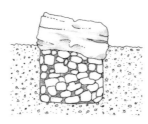

1 *On light ground, dig a trench 20–30cm (8–12in) deep. Fill to 5cm (2in) of the top with rubble.*

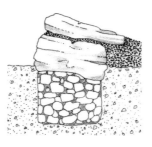

2 *Each layer should slope inwards slightly towards the middle of the bed to add stability.*

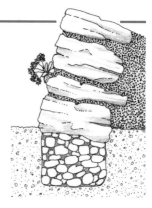

3 *Lay the plant on the rock with its crown facing outwards. Fill in with compost.*

use rocks and the bed is a wide one, a few stepping stones placed on the surface will make it easier when it comes to weeding and general maintenance. As mentioned above, it is easier if the entire bed can be reached from ground level, especially for disabled gardeners.

Planting in wall crevices

Dry stone walls are an attractive feature in any garden. Free-standing walls provide a difficult environment for plants. However, save for stone-crops and houseleeks which can thrive in relatively little soil, or for small ferns which appear by chance and add charm, alpines can be the very devil to establish artificially. Dry stone retaining walls holding back a bank of soil or surrounding a raised bed, on the other hand, can provide a good environment for an exciting selection of alpines. Cracks in such walls are often well-drained and cool, with niches for a variety of trailing and spreading plants, as well as those that form discrete tufts. Walls facing in different directions provide ideal aspects for a great variety of plants. Wall crevices need to be deep enough to connect with the soil or compost behind, downward-sloping and full of compost, without air pockets that would trap roots and prevent them from spreading, so starving them of both moisture and nutrients.

Suitable pockets for plants can be made as construction proceeds and plants can be introduced during the building process (see Making a dry stone retaining wall, below left): this is particularly suitable for plants with large root systems which would be difficult to plant after the wall has been completed. It often transpires, however, that plants have to be introduced in to an existing wall. If the wall is old, it is wise to scrape out the crevice as much as possible and introduce some fresh gritty compost: a rather messy and time-consuming operation. Filter or dribble fresh compost into the crevice using a funnel made of cardboard or plastic, pressing it well in to exclude possible air pockets. Plant your alpines before the crevices are full of compost, using a spatula, widger, small spoon, or even a pencil, to spread the roots carefully as far into the crevice as possible and, at the same time, dribble further compost in. Set the neck of the plant slightly back into the crevice and wedge it in firmly but very carefully with small pieces of rock. This will also help prevent the new compost from being washed out. Both horizontal and vertical crevices can be planted, although soil is more easily eroded from the latter: a large stone wedged in above the crevice will shield the plant and prevent it being washed out.

The choice of suitable plants is surprisingly large, from small hummock- or cushion-forming types, such as *Acantholimon glumaceum* with its spiny grey

PLANTS FOR SHADY CREVICES
Arenaria balearica
Asarina procumbens
Asplenium septentrionale
Corydalis lutea
* C. ochroleuca*
Cymbalaria muralis
* C. pallida*
Haberlea rhodopensis
Phlox adsurgens
* P. × procumbens*
Primula auricula
Ramonda myconi
* R. nathaliae*
Roscoea cautleiodes
Saxifraga cotyledon
Sedum dasyphyllum

Preparing a raised bed

Lightly fork over the base and add a 6–8cm (2¼–3in) layer of rubble or ballast to aid drainage. Cover with inverted turves to prevent compost trickling through and causing a blockage. Fill the bed to 2cm (¾in) of the top with compost, treading each successive load down and firming in well, and leave to settle, particularly if the bed is more than 20cm (8in) deep. Create a rock outcrop on the surface or build up different levels of rocks to provide useful niches for plants. Add a scattering of stone chippings.

PLANTS FOR SUNNY
CREVICES
Acantholimon glumaceum
Antirrhinum molle
 A. sempervirens
*Campanula
 portenschlagiana*
Ceterach officinarum (fern)
Dianthus deltoides
Erinus alpinus
Erodium corsicum
Genista procumbens
Jovibarba hirsuta
Lewisia cotyledon
 L. 'George Henley'
Onosma alborosea
 O. echioides
Primula marginata
Saponaria ocymoides
Saxifraga longifolia
 S. paniculata
 S. 'Southside Seedling'
 S. 'Tumbling Waters'
Sedum acre
 S. cauticola
 S. dasyphyllum
Sempervivum ciliosum
 S. montanum
 S. tectorum
Verbascum dumulosum

leaves and small pink flowers, and the soft tufts of yellow *Corydalis lutea* which seems to be in flower almost throughout the year, to rosette species such as the succulent-leaved lewisias and shade-loving ramondas. Trailing growths are provided by red-, pink- or white-flowered *Dianthus deltoides* and *Saponaria ocymoides* with its bright pink blossoms. Do not be tempted, nevertheless, to overplant and so obscure too much of the attractive stonework.

When choosing plants, give preference to young specimens rather than large, pot-bound ones, which are likely to suffer severe root damage as they are crammed into the crevice; they will establish better if most of the existing compost is gently knocked away from their roots just before planting.

Newly planted walls need careful attention: plants should not be allowed to dry out and must be sprayed and watered regularly, especially during dry weather. They should also be checked to see that they remain firmly in their crevices. Once established, the roots will delve deep into the wall and stabilize the soil-filled crevices, sometimes even seeding into other suitable cracks in the wall.

Planting a raised bed

As there is a huge choice of suitable plants available for raised beds, it is best to avoid everyday alpines that will grow almost anywhere in the garden: space on raised beds is at a premium and is better devoted to the choicer and more difficult types. Avoid any plants that are invasive and spreading, especially those that have underground runners – for example *Campanula cochleariifolia*, *Cymbalaria pallida* and *Potentilla cuneata*, all of them charming alpines but a curse on a raised bed. At the same time, beware any plants that are likely to seed around prolifically (see page 24). Choose bulbs with care, as any large leaves will not only look untidy but will also sprawl on to choicer alpines and may damage them. The final choice is obviously a personal one: the bed could be devoted to a group of saxifrages or drabas, or to a mixture of different alpines.

Colour is an important feature of many small alpines and raised beds can provide spots of interest from late winter onwards. *Primula marginata* thrives in such situations with primrose flowers in white, pink, lilac or purple. Mats of leathery, deep green leaves and trumpet flowers of the most vivid blue characterize *Gentiana acaulis*, surely one of the finest alpines in our gardens and guaranteed to attract attention. Soft grey leaves and pale pink flowers are the main attractions of *Asperula suberosa* contrasting well with the lime-encrusted leaf rosettes of *Saxifraga grisebachii* 'Wisley' with its extraordinary velvety red flower-spikes.

The mountain avens (*Dryas octopetala*) have extensive evergreen mats which produce solitary white flowers in the spring followed by attractive fluffy fruit-heads in the summer. The ordinary form is too vigorous for a raised bed but the dwarf variant 'Minor' is ideal: planted close to the edge the growths will creep over the sides softening the hard outline of the bed. *Globularia repens* will also do the same, rewarding with a show of blue powderpuff

ABOVE LEFT *A prolific
spreader,* Campanula
portenschlagiana *will
infest every crevice in a
dry stone wall, repaying
the gardener with a
splendid show of flowers
for many weeks.*

ABOVE RIGHT *A retaining dry
stone wall provides niches
for crevice plants and
ferns which will often sow
themselves into the
cracks. Colourful alpines
decorate the top of this
wall, spilling over the
edge in places to mask the
harsh line of the stone.*

are exceptional in their floriferousness and attract a host of butterflies. The flat forms of the *Dianthus* contrast nicely with the more open airy growths of *Linum suffruticosum* var. *salsoloides* 'Nanum' with its delicate white flowers with a deep violet centre which unfurl during the day.

Most dwarf bulbs are too leafy for raised beds but some are sufficiently restricted in foliage to make their inclusion worthwhile. One of the finest is *Oxalis adenophylla* with neatly cut grey leaves and satiny flowers in shades of pink. Some of the small tulip species make bold groups to enliven the spring display – bright red *Tulipa linifolia* or yellow and white *T. tarda* are worth considering. On a smaller scale the rather unusual, yet readily available, forms of *Rhodohypoxis baurii*, with their small tufts of leaves and three-lobed flowers in whites, pinks and reds fit in well with the cushion and tufted alpines; they must be protected from excessive winter wet.

Height on the raised bed can be achieved by planting dwarf conifers or small shrubs. Of the conifers the standard choice of *Juniperus communis* 'Compressa' is difficult to beat with its upright columnar habit.

It is a good idea to plant a number of larger plants, especially dwarf shrubs, so as to give a backbone to the structure: position these first and then plan the rest of the planting around them, taking time off occasionally to stand back and view the overall effect. If a particular plant looks out of place, it can easily be moved at this stage. Plant each alpine with care, scooping out a hollow and spreading out the roots before pushing back the compost and firming the plant well in. Shrubs and dwarf trees should be planted at the same depth at which they were growing in their pots. The crowns of the smaller alpines, especially the cushion types, should stand clear of the compost by 1–2cm (½–¾in) to allow for a top-dressing of rock chippings (see page 28).

Once planting is completed, water the bed thoroughly and take care not to let it dry out too much during the first few weeks as the plants establish themselves. The finished bed may need to be protected in winter (see page 26). Caring for raised beds is included in the discussion of routine maintenance in the chapter on Creating a garden for alpines.

flowers in early summer. Another good edge plant is *Anthemis montana* with attractive grey leaves and white daisies over a long season.

Saxifrages should be an important element on any raised bed, many being compact and accommodating plants. There is a huge selection from which to choose, from flat ground-huggers like *Saxifraga oppositifolia* which has blooms of pink or purple in early spring, to imposing large-rosetted types like *S.* 'Tumbling Waters' or 'Southside Seedling' which both produce large panicles of flowers during the summer months. But there are many small cushion species of great charm and in almost any colour – try for instance *S. burseriana* 'Crenata' (white), *S.* 'Faldonside' (pale yellow), *S.* × *anglica* 'Myra' (rosy-carmine) or 'Winifred' (carmine-pink).

Early summer is an excellent time with many choice alpines coming into flower. The various forms of *Dianthus alpinus* with pink, red or white flowers

A sunny dry stone wall

Dry stone walls can be greatly enhanced by alpines to provide interest throughout the year. Not all alpines are suitable for wall crevices and only trial and error can show which are the best in different regions. This plan is shown in mid-summer.

1 *Acantholimon glumaceum*: cushion-forming; spiny grey leaves and small pink flowers early to mid-summer.

2 *Campanula cochleariifolia* (fairy's thimble): delicate leafy stems with little nodding blue bell flowers late spring to mid-summer.

3 *Ceterach officinarum* (rustyback fern): small, sun-loving fern which will wedge itself into the tightest crevice; grows to 20cm (8in).

4 *Erinus alpinus* (fairy foxglove): mass of pink, red or white flowers in late spring and often a few later in the season; once established, will seed itself into crevices.

5 *Lewisia cotyledon*: succulent-leaved crevice plant flowering in late spring to early summer; brash colours from white to pink, apricot, orange, red and yellow.

6 *Penstemon newberryi* (mountain pride): evergreen mats with dull green, leathery leaves and bright, rose-pink flowers in mid-summer.

7 *Saponaria ocymoides* (rock soapwort): mat-forming with lax stems and bright pink flowers from mid-spring to late summer.

8 *Saxifraga longifolia*: single symmetrical, lime-encrusted rosettes which grow gradually larger over the years before producing arching panicles of a myriad of small white flowers; plant dies after flowering and will need replacing but it is well worth the effort.

9 *Sedum acre* (wall pepper): succulent-leaved; mass of bright yellow flowers early to mid-summer.

10 *Sempervivum montanum* (mountain houseleek): succulent leaf rosettes; reddish-purple flowers through summer.

A shady dry stone wall

A dry stone wall in a shady part of the garden might appear to offer little planting potential but this is simply not so. They provide niches which many ferns and shade-loving alpines adore and are cooler and dry out less quickly than those exposed to the sun. This plan is illustrated in late spring.

1 *Arenaria balearica*: thrives in the moister crevices, creeping out like moss over the surface of the rocks; smothered in small, white flowers in spring.

2 *Asplenium trichomanes* (maidenhair spleenwort): neat fern with narrow fronds of rounded, bright green leaflets set along shiny black stalks; 10–25cm (4–10in) spread.

3 *Corydalis lutea*: ferny grey leaves; succession of yellow flowers from late spring until autumn; prolific seeder.

4 *Cymbalaria muralis* (ivy-leaved toadflax): slender shoots will trail down the wall, tiny lilac or violet snapdragon flowers during summer.

5 *Haberlea rhodopensis*: along with the ramonda, perhaps the most exciting and eye-catching plant for a shady crevice; pink, lavender, blue or white flowers from late spring to early summer; drought-resistant.

6 *Iris cristata*: grassy clumps with small iris flowers in blue, lilac or white from late spring to early summer.

7 *Pratia pedunculata*, syn. *Lobelia pedunculata*: small-leaved, spreading plant; numerous small, mauve-pink flowers in summer and early autumn.

8 *Ramonda myconi*: rosette-forming crevice plant with flat flowers of blue, mauve or pink which are produced in late spring to early summer; drought-resistant.

Growing alpines in containers

SUN-LOVERS FOR
TROUGHS
Anchusa caespitosa
Asperula suberosa
Dianthus alpinus
Draba aizoides
Gentiana verna 'Angulosa'
Globularia repens
Helianthemum oelandicum
    subsp. *alpestre*
Iris cristata
Linum suffruticosum var.
    salsoloides 'Nanum'
Paraquilegia anemonoides
Phlox douglasii
Potentilla nitida
Primula marginata
Saxifraga cochlearis
    'Minor'
    S. cotyledon
    S. paniculata
Sempervivum
    arachnoideum

DWARF SHRUBS FOR
TROUGHS
Chamaecyparis obtusa
Daphne arbuscula,
    D. petraea 'Grandiflora'
Juniperis communis
    'Compressa'
Salix reticulata

Troughs, sinks and other containers make excellent environments for alpine plants, providing irresistible opportunities to create miniature alpine gardens, each unique in its design and planting. They are also ideal for today's small gardens and terraces. Suitable containers may be made of stone, glazed earthenware, concrete, unglazed terracotta or pseudo-rock (hypertufa). Whatever the material and the size, it is essential that they be frostproof and allow for sufficient drainage.

Old stone sinks and troughs, now greatly sought after by alpine growers, have become both scarce and expensive. Modern stone or reconstituted stone sinks are available from some sources, including a few garden centres, and are every bit as good as the older ones, although generally very expensive and lacking the patina of old age. However, it is perfectly possible to make sinks and troughs fairly simply and certainly far more cheaply by a do-it-yourself method. Straight concrete is the most basic option, although the finished product is likely to look artificial and rather stark in the garden. Only a little extra effort is required to make a much more attractive trough from hypertufa which gives the effect of rock, ages quickly and soon acquires the mosses and lichens that can be such an interesting feature of real rock. Hypertufa is made from one part by volume coarse sand or fine grit, one part cement and one to two parts sphagnum peat, all mixed into a fairly stiff paste.

Troughs can be made from hypertufa using a wooden box or stiff cardboard mould with a smaller box placed inside, wire netting and sand (see Making a hypertufa trough, below right). The surfaces of the boxes should first be coated with oil to prevent the hypertufa from sticking to them. At each stage the hypertufa should be firmed down well to ensure that all air pockets are eliminated. Cover the finished trough with plastic and protect it from any frost until it has set (this usually takes about a week).

Hypertufa troughs can be made any size but it is important to remember that the larger ones can be very heavy to move, even when empty, so that it is often best to create them *in situ* in the garden. White glazed sinks, which can be bought fairly easily and cheaply but which have a rather stark and unsympathetic appearance, can also be coated with hypertufa to look very like a real stone sink. The surface should be clean and dry and it is best to roughen it by scouring it all over with a tile or glass cutter or by carefully chipping it with a hammer and chisel. Next, coat the surface with a bonding agent such as epoxy resin, then add the hypertufa by hand, preferably wearing gloves, moulding it on to the sides of the sink to a depth of about 2cm (¾in) and pushing it firmly down. Only the top 2–3cm (¾–1¼in) of the inner surface of the sink need be covered, as the trough will be filled with compost and the inner surface obscured. Once it has dried, roughly six to seven days later, the surface can be roughened with a stiff wire brush and further aged by coating it with a solution of permanganate of potash, liquid manure or milk to encourage the growth of mosses and lichens.

Siting

Containers are best placed in an open sunny or partially shaded position that is not exposed to fierce winds. Paved or gravelled areas are ideal; grass presents more problems as it is difficult to mow round containers. They must be stable, with no possibility of them toppling over, especially if small children or pets are about. Sinks and small troughs look best if they are raised off the ground by about 30–45cm (1–1½ft) on a firm stone or brick base, designed so as not to block the drainage holes. Coated glazed sinks with a single drainage hole should be tilted slightly so that any excess water will run away through the hole.

The compost should be a standard alpine mixture of one part by volume of sterilized loam (a soil-based potting compost will do), one part peat, peat substitute or sifted garden compost and one part washed sharp grit. This makes a free-draining compost, rich in organic matter, that most alpines will enjoy. The compost can also vary from container to

container in order to accommodate different groups of plants with, for instance, a lime-free medium for acid-loving plants or a higher percentage of organic matter for moisture-loving subjects such as ferns. Each container can also enjoy its own mini-environment and become a self-contained miniature garden in its own right.

Filling the container

Cover the drainage holes with flower pot shards or fine wire mesh. Place up to 9cm (3½in) of coarse grit or stone chippings in the base of the container, followed by an equal layer of fibrous peat or peat substitute. Then top up with the compost, ensuring that it is firmed down well.

Terracotta pans are perfect for miniature alpine gardens. Here a collection of encrusted saxifrages (left) and a mass of houseleeks (right) create a delightful display.

Making a hypertufa trough

Place a 5–7cm (2–2¾in) layer of hypertufa mixture in the base of the larger box and reinforce the base and sides with wire netting. Add a 5–7cm (2–2¾in) layer of hypertufa and make several 2–3cm (¾–1¼in) holes for drainage (see 1, right). Fill the smaller box with sand to make it stable and insert into the larger box. Fill the cavity between the two boxes with hypertufa (see 2, right). When the hypertufa has set, remove the moulds carefully, using a hammer and chisel if necessary (see 3, right).

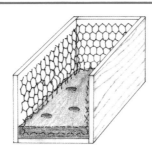

1 Use short pieces of broom handle to create drainage holes in the base. Knock them out once the hypertufa has set.

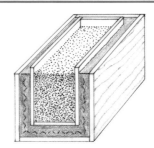

2 Fill the cavity between the two boxes with hypertufa so that the wire netting is more or less equidistant from the walls.

3 Roughen up the outside of the trough with a stiff wire brush to create a more natural look and round off the sharp corners.

A shady trough

Ferns are an obvious choice for a shady trough and, although they do not flower, they provide extra interest in their form, subtleness of colour and in the various divisions of their unfurled fronds. A trough devoted entirely to suitable small ferns can provide a cool 'corner' in a shade-dappled part of the garden. There are no better plants for a shady trough than the ramondas and haberleas. Although close cousins of the african violet, they are completely hardy, thriving in the cool shade and moisture. This plan is illustrated in mid- to late spring.

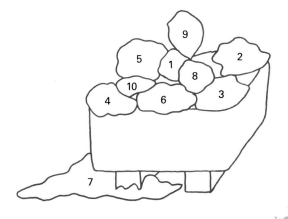

1 *Adiantum pedatum* var. *subpumilum*: elegant, semi-evergreen fern with daintily dissected, bright green fronds; 10–15cm (4–6in).
2 *Asplenium trichomanes* (maidenhair spleenwort): narrow fronds of rounded, bright green leaflets; 10–25cm (4–10in).
3 *Cassiope* 'Edinburgh': dwarf shrub growing to a height of 20cm (8in) with tiny, scale-like leaves and pearly white bell flowers in late spring and early summer.
4 *Gentiana ternifolia*: spreading stems with slender, pointed leaves in twos or threes; blue trumpet flowers towards the end of summer.

5 *Haberlea rhodopensis*: narrow leaves and rosettes which build up into substantial hummocks in time; pale lilac, trumpet-shaped flowers late spring to early summer.
6 *Iris cristata*: makes grassy clumps with small iris flowers in blue, lilac or white late spring to early summer; a charming plant which is prone to slug damage when grown in the open ground.
7 *Pratia pedunculata*, syn. *Lobelia pedunculata*: small-leaved spreading plant with many mauve-pink flowers which are produced in summer and early autumn.

8 *Ramonda myconi*: flat rosettes of deep green leaves divide slowly, producing mauve, pink or blue cup-shaped flowers in late spring to early summer; this species of *Ramonda* is the easiest to grow and the most readily available.
9 *Sisyrinchium douglasii*: large, bell-shaped flowers in satiny purple or white at the first hint of spring; thread-like stems and leaves; 15–25cm (6–10in).
10 *Trillium rivale*: white, three-petalled flowers, often spotted or flushed pink inside, in early spring; plant spreads slowly but is in no way invasive.

1 *Androsace hirtella*: cushion-forming plant which will remain small and bun-like for many years; white flowers in spring.

2 *Daphne arbuscula*: evergreen shrub, forming a low mound, 10–15cm (4–6in) with clusters of rich pink flowers in mid-spring to early summer; greatly resents disturbance.

3 *Dianthus alpinus*: flat cushions of dark green, oblong leaves; huge pink or purplish flowers in summer.

4 *Gentiana verna* (spring gentian): bright blue flowers mid- to late spring; short-lived but easily propagated from seed or cuttings; a whole trough devoted to this species is extremely eyecatching.

5 *Globularia repens*: evergreen shrub forming a mat of tiny leaves; powder-blue flowers in late spring and early summer.

6 *Juniperus communis* 'Compressa': dwarf, slow-growing conifer making a dense, pointed column of grey-green foliage; to 1.5m (5ft).

7 *Oxalis* 'Ione Hecker': one of the few bulbous plants suitable for troughs; forms tufts of neatly cut grey leaves with funnel-shaped, purple-blue flowers which open in the sunshine mid- to late spring.

8 *Rhodohypoxis baurii*: discrete tufts of short, spear-shaped leaves and bright flowers in a range of colours from white to pink, red and purple in spring and early summer.

9 *Saxifraga cochlearis* 'Minor': lime-encrusted rosettes; light sprays of small white flowers in early summer; 20–25cm (8–10in) in flower.

10 *Saxifraga paniculata*: interesting lime-encrusted rosettes; arching sprays, 30cm (1ft) long or more, of white or cream flowers in early summer.

11 *Sisyrinchium* 'E K Balls': grass-like tufts; charming blue flowers early to mid-summer.

A well-filled trough provides a colourful display in early summer. Saxifrages (Saxifraga 'Southside Seedling' on the right) vie with pink thrift and succulent, rosetted Lewisia cotyledon which comes in an enviable range of colours. Viola 'Prince Henry' is planted behind.

PLANTS FOR SHADED TROUGHS
*requires acid soil
Arenaria balearica
Corydalis ambigua
C. cashmeriana
Cyclamen coum
*Gentiana sino-ornata**
*G. ternifolia**
Haberlea rhodopensis
Hepatica nobilis
Iris cristata
Jeffersonia dubia
Pratia pedunculata
*Primula boothii**
*P. gracilipes**
*P. sonchifolia**
*P. whitei**
Ramonda myconi
R. nathaliae
Rhododendron – very dwarf types only*
*Shortia uniflora**
Sisyrinchium douglasii
Trillium rivale

FERNS
Adiantum pedatum var. *subpumilum*
Asplenium adiantum-nigrum
A. dareoides
A. septentrionale
A. trichomanes
Ceterach officinarum
Polypodium hesperium
Woodsia alpina
W. polystichoides

Troughs and other containers look best if they contain several good sized pieces of rock, preferably limestone, sandstone or tufa. Rocks should be well bedded into the compost to at least one third of their depth and can be arranged so as to provide crevices and hollows as well as shady corners and other niches to suit a wide range of plants.

Planting containers

It is important to choose subjects that complement one another, are not too invasive and are suitable for the compost in a particular container. Tufted and cushion-forming alpines are ideal, small bulbs and carpeting plants are generally less satisfactory. The routine maintenance of containers planted with alpines is discussed in the earlier chapter on Creating a garden for alpines.

Containers in shady positions

While most alpines enjoy a bright airy position in full sun and will not tolerate too much shade, others revel in cool shade and moister soils. A trough or sink placed in a shady part of the garden can therefore be just as interesting as those in sunny positions, and indeed it can be very effective in cheering up an otherwise rather dull corner. Shady courtyards and terraces can also benefit greatly from the clever placing of a well-planted container. The best position is a sheltered, open site away from overhanging trees and drips from the eaves of buildings which could damage the plants.

Many of these plants require a moister compost than the majority of most alpines: three parts peat or peat substitute to one or two parts sterilized loam and one part coarse grit is a suitable mix; it can be made acid or alkaline depending on whether or not you want to grow acid-loving plants (see page 36). Many ferns enjoy moist shaded conditions and some of the smaller ones make excellent container plants, the subtle difference in the colouring and delicate forms of the leaves providing interest in the garden for many months of the year.

It is important not to forget to water shaded containers for, although they will not dry out as fast as those positioned in sunny parts of the garden, during spells of dry weather and even during the winter months, they will lose humidity and the plants – especially ferns – will soon begin to die if left unwatered for any length of time.

Alpines and tufa

Tufa is an extraordinary rock, formed from thick deposits of calcium carbonate; it is not only extremely light for its bulk but also very easy to drill holes into. Furthermore, it is porous, taking up water rather like a sponge through an elaborate system of minute capillaries. For all these reasons it is particularly useful for growing certain types of alpines, especially the choicer cushion-forming and tufted species. Indeed, it provides a self-contained medium in which to grow alpine plants. Unfortunately, it is also rather scarce and not cheap but just a few good-sized pieces placed in a trough or on a raised bed can provide invaluable additional niches for plants. Several haulage firms will supply large quantities of tufa but smaller supplies should be bought from specialist alpine plant nurseries, which often sell it piece by piece.

Freshly quarried tufa is yellowish, soft and crumbly but the surface quickly weathers to become hard, pitted and rather grey. Because it is expensive to buy, pieces of tufa are best used in the garden for a special feature or for growing some of the smaller and more select alpines.

However you choose to use it, the balance between the amount of tufa above and below the soil surface is critical. If it is too deeply buried, it will take up too much water from the ground and become saturated but, on the other hand, if it is not buried deep enough, it will dry out too quickly. For most purposes tufa blocks are best buried to a fifth or a quarter of their depth: this seems to give the best balance for a wide range of alpines.

Tufa is best placed in an open, airy, well-lit position, so as to provide niches of varying aspects to suit different plants. Once you have positioned it, leave it for a while, about three to four weeks, to settle down and weather a bit, hosing it down to remove any excess loose or soft material clinging to the blocks. Some pieces of tufa are naturally softer than others but most will soon weather to a resistant core. Fine crumbly tufa can be added to the compost in which the tufa is set, or used in potting mixtures in the alpine house.

Holes for crevice plants can be bored in tufa with a drill and 2.5–3cm (1–1¼in) bit or simply with a strong old screwdriver or chisel. They should be about 7–8cm (2¾–3in) deep, inclined downwards, and no closer than 10cm (4in) to each other. Once drilled, tufa is best soaked for 24 hours before planting (see Planting in a tufa crevice, page 84).

More substantial lumps of tufa can be used to make a tufa garden or cliff, which can become an interesting and unusual feature to accommodate a surprising range of alpines (see Plants for a tufa block in full sun, page 85). These can be planted in spring, early summer or early autumn, provided the plants have time to settle in before winter arrives. If they are planted too late, frosts tend to push the young alpines out of their holes in the tufa, so it is wise to make regular checks in order to firm them back into

USING TUFA

Tufa can be used in a number of ways:

● A large piece, say 90cm × 1.5m (3 × 5ft), can be used as a free-standing block. Alternatively, a number of smaller pieces can be arranged together to create a similar effect.

● Pieces of tufa can be placed in a shallow trough to create a small tufa garden or used to make a feature on a raised bed.

● At the other extreme, elaborate (and expensive) tufa cliffs can be made, with a protective roof to exclude the worst of the rain and frost.

Saxifrages, especially the kabschia types, are ideal subjects for tufa. Saxifraga 'Myra' blooms in early spring, along with a host of related cultivars in a wide range of colours.

PLANTS FOR TUFA

Anchusa caespitosa
Androsace ciliata
  A. hirtella
Campanula piperi
  C. tommasiniana
  C. zoysii
Dianthus pindicola
  D. simulans
Draba polytricha
Edraianthus pumilio
Helichrysum milfordiae
Leontopodium nivale
Paraquilegia anemonoides
Petrocallis pyrenaica
Physoplexis comosa
Phyteuma orbiculare
Ramonda nathaliae
Raoulia lutescens
Saxifraga caesia
  S. 'Faldonside'
  S. 'Gem'
  S. marginata
  S. retusa
  S. 'Winifred'
Viola cazorlensis
  V. delphinantha

place. Plants settle in most readily and are best able to cope with the upheaval of being moved if most of the compost is removed from around their roots. Only young, vigorous alpine plants should be selected; do not attempt to cram the roots of a mature plant into a tight tufa hole.

Until they become established, alpines planted in tufa need special care to make sure they do not dry out too rapidly, especially on hot sunny days when they may require regular watering. Once they have settled in, their roots will begin to delve deep within the tufa to seek out moisture and nutrients. At this stage watering is mostly unnecessary except during prolonged dry spells. It is sometimes difficult to tell whether tufa needs watering, but a check of the surrounding compost will generally give a useful indication. Watering should be done gently in order to avoid buffeting the plants too roughly and damaging them.

Some plants are bound not to survive and any that fail can be removed, the hole scooped out and a replacement plant introduced. Young healthy plants, whether pot-grown, newly rooted cuttings or even seedlings, are the most likely to succeed. Healthy plants can live happily in tufa for many years, often growing slowly, tightly and in character – this is especially true of some of the cushion alpines which, under less lean conditions, tend to grow loose and unattractive.

Any weeds should be removed from tufa quickly, before they have a chance to become established, otherwise they may be difficult to remove without delving deep into the rock with a knife. Moss, liverworts and pearlworts (*Sagina* species) can be a problem, especially if they become well established, swamping young or slow-growing alpines and quickly killing them. Remove them by hand, scraping the surface of the tufa with an old knife or spatula. Moss and liverworts can also be killed using a proprietary moss-killer. Use them with care, however, as although they are unlikely to damage most alpines, they cannot be guaranteed not to do so.

Planting in tufa

Tufa is for discrete little alpines, for the more unusual types that thrive best in more specialized conditions. There is no point in covering expensive tufa blocks in the commoner or easy alpines that will thrive perfectly well on the average rock garden. Rather, concentrate on the choicer, slower-growing and rarer species and cultivars which not only look attractive on tufa but also respond so well to being grown on it.

A large block of tufa will accommodate a surprising variety of alpines of which those with a cushion form are the most delightful. *Androsace ciliata* forms perfect tight little cushions closely smothered in

Planting in a tufa crevice

Insert a little compost into the tufa crevice with a spatula or widger. Knock or wash most of the compost off the plant to expose the roots (see 1, right). Ease the roots into the chosen hole, dribbling in compost around them. Firm the plant in well, taking care not to damage the delicate root system. Wedge the neck of the plant in with suitable small pieces of tufa or rock to prevent the compost being washed away (see 2, right). Keep the tufa moist until the plants have settled in and show obvious signs of renewed growth.

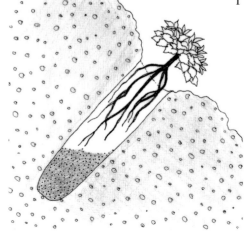
1

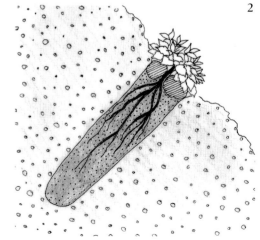
2

bright pink flowers in the spring, whereas *A. hirtella* has grey cushions and scented white flowers much beloved by butterflies emerging after the winter.

Many saxifrages also lend themselves to tufa culture. Not only does the tufa provide them with ideal conditions but they also remain compact and in character. There are many to choose from: *Saxifraga* 'Faldonside' makes domed grey cushions and carries its bright yellow flowers in early spring; *S.* 'Winifred' has flatter, deep green cushions and carmine-pink flowers. Another form is provided by the slow-spreading small mats of *S. retusa* with its eye-catching, rose-red blooms. Most of the small, cushioned saxifrages prefer to be shielded from hot midday sun which tends to scorch the foliage.

Specialities are a must on tufa and provide a challenge. *Viola cazorlensis* and *V. delphinantha* are small subshrubby treasures from the mountains of Spain and the Balkans respectively. Both make tufts with thread-like stems and tiny leaves but show off with their perfect little pansy flowers in shades of pink and violet-pink.

An unusual, yet much sought-after, plant is *Physoplexis comosa*, the so-called devil's claw, which forms tufts of rather succulent, coarsely toothed leaves. In early summer low clusters of bottle-shaped flowers appear, violet-blue with a deep purplish-red tip. Provided it is kept clear of winter wet and marauding slugs, it is easy to grow. A charming

companion plant, and equally good slug fodder, is an unusual little bellflower, *Campanula zoysii*, which sports its crimped lavender flowers over a mat of bright shiny green leaves. For a good blue, try growing the smallest of the anchusas, *Anchusa caespitosa*, a rock-dweller from the high mountains of Crete. This low tufted plant has rosettes of rough bristly leaves which contrast with its clusters of large, brilliant blue, forget-me-not-like flowers.

The spaces between adjacent blocks of tufa provide the perfect home for this spring-flowering Saxifraga retusa.

Plants for a tufa block in full sun

Tufa plants should be discreet, slow-growing and non-invasive – small cushion and tufted plants are the most suitable. Even in a sunny position, a large block of tufa will present various aspects, some in full sun, others in half-shade or complete shade. Ramondas and ferns are perfect for the shadier, cooler niches, while many of the cushion-type alpines prefer sunnier aspects.

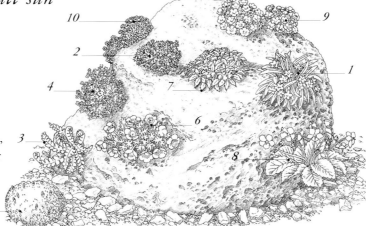

1 *Anchusa caespitosa*
2 *Androsace hirtella*
3 *Ceterach officinarum*
4 *Draba polytricha*
5 *Gypsophila aretioides*
6 *Paraquilegia anemonoides*
7 *Physoplexis comosa*
8 *Ramonda nathaliae*
9 *Saxifraga burseriana* 'Gloria'
10 *Saxifraga* 'Jenkinsiae'

THE ALPINE HOUSE

Not only does the alpine house provide more easily controllable conditions for difficult plants, like the numerous cultivars of the spring-flowering Primula allionii *or the bright hummocks of dionysias or androsaces, but it can also help extend the flowering season to provide colour throughout the year. In winter periods, when the weather is cold and gardening out-of-doors difficult, the alpine house becomes a haven, with the first bulbs coming into bloom early in mid-winter followed by a succession of alpines and other dwarf bulbs.*

The alpine house provides the ideal environment for a great variety of small, rare and difficult alpine plants. Especially valuable are those that flower during winter and early spring such as the delightful Primula allionii cultivars, alpine violas, saxifrages and Fritillaria aurea, shown here neatly potted on the alpine bench.

Growing alpines under glass

This well-ventilated alpine house provides much colour in late winter and spring. A collection of succulent lewisias, moisture-loving ramondas, haberleas and various bulbs is plunged in a sandbed which allows for easier viewing and prevents plants from drying out too quickly.

In the wild, alpines grow primarily in open, airy habitats. What they most hate in cultivation is an enclosed and dank atmosphere with little or no air circulation. To reproduce the plant's natural environment as closely as possible, the alpine house, essentially an unheated glasshouse, must be open and airy which excludes most ordinary glasshouses. One or two firms manufacture specially designed alpine houses but these are extremely expensive. Instead, you can select a glasshouse design that can be easily modified by replacing existing glass with extra ventilators. Most manufacturers should be able to advise on the type and amount of extra ventilation that is possible on a given model – the aim being as much ventilation as possible. Ventilators should be set along the sides of the house at ground level, in the middle section at about waist height and also in the roof of the house to allow for a continuous sideways and upwards flow of air through the structure. In the best alpine houses a continuous line of ventilators runs the full length of the house on each side. As a rough guide, ventilators should take up at least 25 per cent of the glass area of the house.

Siting

An open, level, sunny site, without any overhanging trees is essential for a successful alpine house, avoiding frost pockets or a damp situation which hollows in the garden sometimes create. A north-south orientation that can take advantage of maximum light to all parts of the alpine house is ideal but not essential. Also important to consider is the position of the structure within the garden. It should be easily accessible and harmonize with the rest of the garden as far as possible, so think about its relationship to existing features and to the overall plan of the garden. This is more difficult with metal-alloy structures which stand out starkly and unsympathetically from their surroundings and never seem to mellow with age. Wooden houses are generally less offensive to the eye and tend to blend in more readily with the garden landscape but they are usually more expensive. Most of the major glasshouse manufacturers will erect the framework for you. This service is usually efficient and relatively cheap and may be worth considering.

Choosing pots

Alpines can be grown equally successfully in clay or plastic pots. Many alpine growers prefer clay pots, however, because their porosity allows a certain amount of water to pass through the pot walls, which is particularly important for pots placed in a sand plunge. In addition, clay pots are known to keep the roots of the plants cooler and this is of great benefit to most alpines.

Pots come in various shapes and sizes. Standard pots, half pots and pans are all useful for growing alpines, as well as the extra long pots known as long toms which allow extra depth for very long and penetrating roots. Many alpines have a large root to top-growth ratio and require a lot of space in which to develop. This often means frequent potting on into a larger pot, particularly when the plants are in active growth. Pans are most suitable for seeds and young plants or succulents such as houseleeks (*Sempervivum* species) which have a small root system. Half pots and standard pots will suit many alpines, the latter for those with more vigorous root systems.

Planting and repotting

The steps to follow when planting new plants or repotting are the same (see Growing alpines in pots, below). However, some alpines, particularly many of the more specialized cushion species such as dionysias and androsaces, require careful potting to prevent the vulnerable base and neck of the cushion from becoming too damp and rotting. The normal procedure is followed when potting these plants but you do have to ensure that the neck of the plant is bedded in a layer of grit. Pieces of rock fragment are then wedged carefully under the collar of the cushion to lift it off the surface of the compost.

Delicate dionysias present a real challenge to growers. Suitable only for the alpine house, they require very careful nurturing. Here, Dionysia bryoides *from the mountains of south-west Iran is shown double potted. Water is applied only to the outer pot to prevent the plant becoming too wet.*

Growing alpines in pots

Place a piece of perforated zinc or clay crocks over the drainage hole and insert the plant. Fill with compost to within 2cm (¾in) of the rim of the pot and top-dress with coarse grit, tucking it carefully under the neck of the plant (see 1, right).

The neck of a specialized cushion species should be bedded in a thick (1–2cm/½–¾in) layer of coarse grit (see 2, right).

For double potting, place the potted alpine in a larger pot, ensuring the rims of the two pots are at the same level (see 3, right).

Potting and repotting
Half pots and standard pots, of clay or plastic, are suitable for most alpine plants.

Cushion alpines
Wedge pieces of rock under the collar of the cushion to lift it off the surface of the compost.

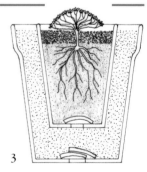

Double potting
Fill the gap between the clay pots with sand. Water is then absorbed through the clay.

Double potting (see Growing alpines in pots, page 89) can be used for those plants that are easily overwatered, such as cushion alpines. This method involves placing the potted alpine inside a larger pot containing sharp sand to ensure a more careful watering regime and keep the vulnerable, exposed parts of the plant free from moisture. Only clay pots can be used. The plant is then simply watered and fed through the sand surround and this ensures that the plant itself is left reasonably dry.

Plants require repotting when they become pot-bound which is often apparent by a slowing-down of growth and by a mass of roots pushing through the drainage hole at the base of the pot. Repotting involves moving the plant into a clean pot one size larger; plants should be knocked out of their old pots with care so as not to damage the delicate root system. After potting or repotting, water the plant thoroughly, preferably by standing it in water.

Displaying plants

There are a number of ways in which to use the alpine house. Where space is limited, one half of the house can be used for propagation and growing while the other half is devoted to display. The plants are usually grown in pots placed on specially constructed staging; the pots can either stand directly on the staging or be plunged up to their rims in sharp sand or another suitable medium, such as hortag. Whatever is chosen, the plunge bed must be well-drained and excess water able to drain away. The advantage of the raised plunge bed is that it evens out the daily and seasonal fluctuations in temperature to some extent and keeps the roots of the plants moist and, more importantly, cool. Wild fluctuations in both temperature and moisture content of the compost can often prove disastrous to alpine plants. Additionally, plants in a plunge bed need less frequent watering and, furthermore, they are better insulated than free-standing ones which are likely to freeze right through during severe winter weather, resulting in damaged plants. An indirect benefit of the raised plunge bed is a useful, partly shaded area beneath for plants that prefer a less sunny environment such as ferns and some cyclamen.

Another way of growing alpines in an alpine house is to plant them directly in beds, either at ground level or raised. This can be very effective for display but is rather wasteful of space as fewer plants can be accommodated in a given area, a situation that may be exacerbated by the fact that plants in beds often grow more vigorously than pot-grown specimens. However, this does allow you to create miniature indoor rock gardens to provide niches for a wide range of different plants. Small rocks or lumps of tufa can be used to enhance the display and provide a more natural-looking setting.

Constructing a raised plunge bed

Several types of aluminium plunge beds are available, but they are expensive to buy. However, their advantage is that they are strong and quick and easy to put up. You can construct suitable beds far more cheaply using bricks and well-preserved wood (see Making a raised plunge bed, below right). Whatever materials you use, they must be strong enough to support the great weight of plunge material as well as the pots once the bed is fully laden.

It is usual for the raised plunge bed to run the full length of the alpine house on one or both sides and even across the end, if required. Its height should ideally be at about waist level for ease of access and maintenance – generally about 75–90cm (2½–3ft). The width of the bed depends much on the width of the house but anything over 90cm (3ft) wide will be difficult for access. For disabled gardeners, especially those who are confined to a wheelchair, the height and width of staging is clearly critical and details are best worked out carefully on paper before construction starts. The path width between staging is also critical, for too narrow a space makes access and manoeuvrability tricky.

Breeze blocks, brick pillars or walls provide much better support for the bed than wood but require adequate concrete foundations to support the weight they are to bear. Short transverse walls, the width of the staging, can be constructed at intervals of about 1.5m (5ft). It is essential that the tops of these are exactly level with one another, otherwise the staging will be uneven and a difficult foundation on which to construct the plunge bed.

Tulipa linifolia
This dainty dwarf tulip is one of the finest in cultivation. Its shimmering, scarlet flowers resemble satin ribbon and open out flat in bright, spring sunshine. In the wild it inhabits the dry steppes and rocky hills of Turkestan where many of the ancestors of the modern garden tulip may be found.

For the plunge tray you can use wood – cedarwood or deal is particularly good and can be treated with a suitable preservative from time to time – which will last for many years if properly looked after. Brace the floor of the tray with crosspieces to counteract any bowing tendency caused by the weight of the pots and plunge material. The wood should be sufficiently thick, about 2–3cm (¾–1½in). Build up the sides to about 15cm (6in), nailing or screwing the pieces into place. The open tray can be continuous or broken up into smaller areas by cross walls installed above the supports, which will offer further stability and provide compartments for different groups of alpines or, perhaps, different plunge materials. Line the completed trays with polythene which helps to preserve the timber beneath but perforate it at intervals to allow excess water to drain away.

Plunge materials

Sharp or builder's sand is an ideal plunge medium but it is very heavy when moist. Sharp sand has the advantage of holding a good balance of water and air and allowing the plants to take up adequate moisture when required. It also holds up well when a pot is removed making it easier to replace the pot. The disadvantage is that after a while the surface of the sand becomes clogged with algae and mosses and sometimes liverworts which look unpleasant and can harbour pests and diseases. An alternative is hortag–

clay granules, which are attractive, long lasting and rather lighter than sand for a given volume. Its disadvantage is that it is quite expensive to buy and collapses into the hole as a pot is removed, thus making it rather difficult to re-insert pots in the plunge bench. Other suitable materials include fine pea gravel and granite chippings if these are available. Never use coastal sand: it is often very salty and would undoubtedly damage most plants.

Making a raised plunge bed

Raised plunge beds can be made quite cheaply from bricks and wood. The bricks provide good support while deal or cedarwood can be used for the plunge tray. Where space is at a premium, a second plunge tray on the ground is useful for plants going through a resting period or for those that need less light, such as ferns. Plants should be plunged so that the rims of their pots are clear by about 2–4cm (¾–1½in). This is less critical for pots with a diameter greater than 20cm (8in).

Lewisia tweedyi is an excellent alpine house plant with flamboyant flowers in pink, apricot or white in the spring. Plants should be treated like bulbs – watered in winter but kept bone dry in summer.

Shading

Despite the fact that most alpines prefer as much light as possible, strong sunlight can scorch some plants during spring and early summer when they are putting on new growth, especially certain softer cushion alpines. In addition, during hot and still weather in mid-summer the temperature in the alpine house may become too high, even with all the ventilators fully open, and some of the plants will suffer as a result. A simple system of shading a part or the whole of the house, therefore, is advisable. Shade netting or wooden slats placed over the glasshouse roof will provide dappled shade. Shading can be put up in the late spring and removed in the early autumn. More expensive are roller blinds or automatic shading systems which can be applied when conditions demand.

Movement of air within the house, especially important during still and damp weather at any season of the year, can be greatly increased by using an electric circulating fan. Some growers use fans all the time, summer and winter.

Watering

Although automatic watering systems are widely available for glasshouses, they are at their best when used in houses with only one or two different kinds of plant for they 'average out' the conditions, treating all the plants equally. For the majority of alpines grown in pots, especially those that are rather more difficult to cultivate, manual watering and feeding is preferable, as it allows the individual needs of each plant to be accommodated. With experience the gardener growing alpines in pots gets to know when or when not to apply water or feed. Plants like *Lewisia tweedyi*, for instance, with succulent leaf rosettes and large, silky flowers, require little or no water from mid-summer until early spring, whereas *Cyclamen graecum* or *C. rohlfsianum*, which flower in autumn, thrive only if given a regime of watering during the autumn until early spring followed by little or no water from late spring and into summer.

Many cushion alpines require most moisture when they are in active growth during spring and summer.

The charming and colourful cushion dionysias generally dislike being watered from overhead as do many soft, hairy alpines; for these, water needs to be dribbled carefully around the edge of the pot to avoid splashing the sensitive plant. Alternatively, you can water the plunge medium and the plant takes up all the water it requires through this; plants grown in clay pots will take up moisture from the plunge through the semi-porous sides of the pot. In any event, to prevent alpines lying in a pool of water overnight which may cause fungal infections and other problems, it is wisest to water plants in the

Shading is vital in the alpine house to help maintain correct temperatures. Shade netting is lightweight, easy to remove when not required and produces the desired dappled effect, allowing in some sunlight which is essential for the majority of alpines.

early morning, especially during sunny weather; this ensures that the plants, but not the compost, are reasonably dry by nightfall.

Hardiness and protection from frost

Hardiness is a term loosely used by gardeners. It seems to imply the capability of different plants to survive low temperatures. Some plants may survive a temperature of say $-10°C$ ($14°F$) while others may not. With alpines the problem is far more complicated. The moisture content of the compost, the dryness of the air, the length of time a plant is subjected to a particular temperature and its state of growth may all affect survival. Severe frosts at the onset of winter, for instance, may do far less damage than similar frosts in late winter when many plants in the alpine house will have commenced active growth. Free-standing pots of alpines are likely to suffer more damage than those in a plunge.

The alpine house brings together under one roof plants from many different regions of the world which often have very different climatic conditions. Most are able to survive freezing with varying amounts of damage, some with no appreciable damage whatsoever, but the critical temperature at which a particular plant is badly damaged or killed varies widely from one species to another.

Frost damage can be limited in various ways. During severe weather close down the ventilators on the alpine house but open them again the moment the weather relents and temperatures pick up. Placing sheets of newspaper on top of the plants can provide a surprising degree of protection from a few degrees of frost and cheap, lightweight, thermal fleeces are a huge benefit. During severe winter weather you can line the inside of the house with thermal bubble-polythene, although as it cuts down airflow it would cause harmful condensation problems at any other time. I have found small paraffin heaters (those types specially designed for glasshouses and conservatories) cheap and efficient and they need to be lit only when the threat of severe frost is apparent. It is important that this type of

heater is well maintained as the paraffin fumes will certainly harm some plants, ferns in particular. Other devices include thermal screens fitted all over the exterior of the house or soil-warming cables installed within a plunge bench or part of it. The advantage of the latter is that all those plants such as tender cyclamen, some of the small narcissi and young and vulnerable seedlings can be placed on the warmed part of the bench. The warming cables need be switched on only when the weather turns nasty; the majority of alpines certainly do not require the luxury of such lavish treatment.

Small narcissi, tulips and fritillarias bring a delightful display of spring colour to the alpine house. After flowering, these plants can be moved to cold frames to dry off for the summer and to make room for other plants coming into bloom.

93

Frames

A useful adjunct to the alpine house is the cold frame, which can accommodate overflow plants. You can treat a frame in much the same way as the alpine house with plunge beds and suitable shading, watering and feeding regimes. If you have more than one frame, you can site them in different places according to the types of plant you wish to grow in them. A sunny, open position is best for the majority of alpines but a frame in a cool, shady position in the garden would be ideal for petiolarid primulas, such as *Primula edgeworthii*, pleione orchids or ferns.

You can grow alpines permanently in frames, bringing them into the alpine house as they come into flower or fruit or when their foliage is at its best. This way you can maintain a continuous display of colour and interest in the alpine house for most of the year. Some alpines in fact do better in frames, where the lights can be removed during the summer, than when they are permanently confined to the alpine house. Many primulas and saxifrages belong in this category.

As most alpine enthusiasts enjoy raising their plants from seed, they find frames extremely useful for plunging newly sown pots of seed and seedlings. Seed often requires cold treatment before it will germinate. Sown in autumn or winter, pots of seed are protected within the cold frame but, at the same time, cold weather can penetrate and break the dormancy to initiate germination the moment temperatures begin to rise in the early spring.

Routine maintenance

For the house and frame
• Clean the glass regularly, especially in autumn, to prevent the build up of dirt and algae and to allow as much light as possible through. Remove dirt between overlapping panes by pushing a plastic plant label carefully between the panes.
• Replace any glass that has been broken and dispose of the broken glass with care.
• Check that all ventilators work properly,

Campanula zoysii is easily recognized by its characteristic, crimped bell flowers. Especially effective in the alpine house, it is a plant for the specialist grower to cherish. Although not particularly difficult to grow, it tends to be short-lived and prone to the depredations of slugs but it is, nevertheless, worth every effort.

Devil's claw (Physoplexis comosa) *is a native of the Dolomites and much sought after by alpine gardeners. In the wild it grows in light crevices of dolomitic limestone. It is a highly desirable plant for the alpine house, flowering in early summer. If grown in frames, it will need to be protected from slugs.*

SOME GOOD ALPINE HOUSE PLANTS
*dwarf shrub

Androsace
  cylindrica × hirtella
  A. vandelii
Campanula morettiana
  C. raineri
  C. rupestris
  C. zoysii
*Clematis marmoraria**
Convolvulus boissieri
*Daphne genkwa**
  *D. jasminea**
  D. petraea
  'Grandiflora' *
Dionysia aretioides
  D. curviflora
  D. involucrata
Draba mollissima
  D. polytricha
Jankaea heldreichii
Lewisia cotyledon
  L. rediviva
  L. tweedyi
Morisia monanthos
Paraquilegia anemonoïdes
Phlox mesoleuca
Physoplexis comosa
Primula allionii and its
  many cultivars
  P. marginata
Ramonda myconi
Raoulia eximea
Sarcocapnos enneaphylla
Saxifraga burseriana
  'Gloria'
  S. diapensioides
  S. poluniniana
  S. tombeanensis
Viola cazorlensis
  V. delphinantha

especially if any autovents are installed.
● During stormy weather close the vents just enough so that water is prevented from being blown in or dripping onto the plants.
● Put shading into place in late spring and remove it in late summer. Choose light shading that allows in ample light so that the plants do not become unnaturally drawn.
● Install fine mesh screens over ventilators and doors to prevent birds or cats entering the house and causing damage.
● Check heaters before the onset of winter to make sure they are in full working order.
● Treat timber houses with preservative or paint every three to four years following the manufacturer's recommendations.

For the plants
● Repot any plant that has become pot-bound. This operation is preferable when plants are in active growth; repot early flowering types after flowering to avoid the risk of spoiling the floral display.
● Propagate plants that have become too large by taking cuttings and, once new plants have become established, dispose of the parent.
● Water regularly and sufficiently through the growing season; put those plants that require a dry summer dormancy to one side.
● Water in the early mornings, especially during dull damp weather, to avoid plants remaining in a pool of water overnight. During hot weather damp down the pathway in the house at midday, if possible, to help reduce temperatures.

- Feed established plants on a regular basis during the growing season. Select a low-nitrogen fertilizer and follow the manufacturer's instructions.
- After flowering remove appropriate plants, such as saxifrages and primulas, to cool frames for the summer, to leave part of the alpine house free for other plants.
- Weed sand plunges regularly to prevent undesirable invasions. Check 'weed' seedlings before digging them up to make sure they are not seedlings of desirable alpines that have self-sown.
- Prevent dead plant material accumulating on the floor or on the staging as this will encourage the build up of pests and diseases.
- Check regularly for pests such as vine weevils, aphids, thrips and red spider mites, especially during the growing season. Systemic insecticides or biological controls should be used to control aphids or thrips. Vine weevil is, however, a bigger problem and although the insecticide chlorophos will give some control, it will not eliminate the pest. Microscopic nematodes (eelworms) are an effective biological control and are available to the alpine gardener.
- In autumn and winter keep a watch out for fungal attacks on the plants. Deal with the first sign of any such attack, especially on cushion plants, as soon as possible, otherwise the infection will quickly spread to other parts of the plant. Apply systemic fungicides, although some alpines do resent their use, often indicated by yellowing leaves. Flowers of sulphur (yellow sulphur) is useful for controlling botrytis and other fungi on precious cushion alpines. Regular, careful removal of dead leaves and flowers will help prevent the spread of fungal infections.
- During winter months clean up plants, especially primulas and campanulas, removing dead or yellowing leaves with a pair of tweezers.
- During severe, frosty weather use heaters to keep the minimum temperature of the house just above freezing. Avoid warming the house too much as this will cause the plants to start into growth prematurely. If necessary, keep the heaters on all day.
- Keep plants moist, not bone dry in the winter. Keeping the plunge moist is normally quite sufficient. Increase the amount of water as plants begin to show signs of renewed growth in the spring.

ABOVE Tulipa aucheriana *is a small and delightful Turkish species, seldom seen in gardens although it is readily available. It thrives in the bulb frame where it will multiply steadily over the years.*

LEFT *Crocuses are ideal bulb frame plants, coming into flower during the winter months when few plants are in bloom.*

Bulb frames

Because bulbs generally require a different growing regime to that of many alpines, alpine gardeners often treat them separately. They can be grown in a section of the alpine house but, more often, they are grown in a frame devoted to the many types of bulbous plant. Crocuses, tulips, irises, narcissi, anemones, cyclamen and fritillarias all belong here. Although a wide range of small bulbs are grown out-of-doors on the rock garden, many require the more specialized treatment that the bulb frame is able to offer. These bulbs really are the reverse of other 'alpines'; most bulbs are summer-dormant, disappearing below ground once they have flowered and set seed. Their native habitats have a primarily Mediterranean type of climate and autumn or winter rains usually bring them into growth. In the wild, shortly after spring, the climate becomes dry and hot and the plants begin to die down, surviving the long, hot, dry summer months below ground as bulbs, corms or tubers.

Essentially a raised bed with a permanent cover, the bulb frame enables close imitation of this cycle of winter moisture followed by summer dryness, allowing the bulbs to ripen and flower properly. It should be at least 50cm (20in) high to allow enough room for some of the taller bulbs. Plant the bulbs either directly into a specially prepared bed or into pots plunged into a sand or grit bed in the frame.

Bulb composts need to be free-draining and gritty. If planted directly into the frame bed, then suitable dividers such as bits of stiff plastic or slate help to keep the different species apart, although care should be taken to prevent them seeding about as they will then quickly muddle the collection. Today many growers place the bulbs in lattice (mesh) pots which they then bury in rows in the frame. This makes it very easy to lift groups of bulbs and prevents them getting lost in the bed.

Plant or pot up bulbs in late summer and autumn, taking care to label each pot or batch carefully. With most bulbs, the first watering can take place in the early autumn to encourage root action. Further water may be needed during mild winters but do not water during cold frosty weather. You can leave the frame open during mild weather but close it again when the weather is frosty. In the early spring open it up to allow rain in and leave it open until the leaves begin to yellow and die down. You can then close the frame, leaving the bulbs without water for the duration of the summer.

Pots of suitable bulbs can be brought into the alpine house from the bulb frame as they come into flower to enhance the general display; many come into flower in the depths of winter or early spring providing a welcome splash of colour at the most inclement time of the year.

SOME SUITABLE BULB
FRAME SUBJECTS
*requires frost protection
Anemone bucharica
    A. petiolulosa
Calochortus albus
    C. luteus
    C. pulchellus
Colchicum hungaricum
    C. triphyllum
Corydalis caucasica 'Alba'
    C. solida 'George P Baker'
Crocus – many species and
    cultivars
*Cyclamen africanum**
    C. graecum
    C. libanoticum
    C. pseudibericum
    *C. rohlfsianum**
    C. trochopteranthum
Gymnospermium albertii
Iris – smaller bulbous
    species, especially
    junos, oncocyclus and
    reticulata types
Fritillaria species
Muscari macrocarpum
    M. moschatum
Narcissus asturiensis
    N. bulbocodium and
    cultivars
    N. cantabricus
Oxalis adenophylla
    O. enneaphylla
    *O. hirta**
    O. purpurea 'Ken Aslet'
Romulea species
Sternbergia candida
    S. lutea
    S. sicula
*Tropaeolum tricolorum**
Tulipa aucheriana
    T. pulchella

Oxalis purpurea 'Ken Aslet' has a mat of attractive silvery grey, clover-like leaves. Rich yellow flowers appear in the autumn and winter. It should be treated like most bulbs and given a dry summer rest.

THROUGH THE SEASONS

Each season in the alpine garden brings its own special rewards — the sight of the first blue gentians of spring, for instance, or the last pink cyclamen of autumn are treasured each year. If it is to remain a lasting joy, however, the alpine garden requires regular attention and maintenance. Planning ahead, even in the gloomy depths of winter, and keeping up with seasonal chores are essential to ensure the best results.

In early summer, this corner of a small rock garden is full of colour. White Achillea ageratifolia *subsp.* aizoon *vies with the varying shades of pink of the fairy foxgloves* (Erinus alpinus), Dianthus *and dark-centred* Geranium cinereum *'Ballerina'. Behind, grey-leaved* Euryops acraeus *is smothered in gold, daisy-like flowers and, even though they are past flowering, the dwarf bearded irises bring additional interest to the garden with their sword-like leaves.*

Winter

Rock gardens and screes burst into colour in spring and early summer, with interest continuing well into the autumn. Winter, in contrast, can seem a dull and uninteresting time out-of-doors with the rock garden looking bleak and craggy. Yet, this need not be so. Dwarf conifers, available in a myriad of contrasting shapes and colours, can be used to add structure and interest during winter. In addition there are useful shrubs that can be planted to enliven the rocks or screes. Pink, red and white forms of *Daphne mezereum* and the bright yellow *D. kamtschatica* var. *jezoensis*, for instance, come into bloom at the approach of mid-winter. Even some small alpines come into flower at this time of year; saxifrages such as the delicate pale pink-flowered cushions of *Saxifraga* 'Jenkinsiae' or yellow-flowered *S.* 'Gregor Mendel' (syn. *S. × apiculata*) are reliable.

For winter colour it is difficult to compete with some of the dwarf bulbs which add interest to pockets between rocks. The pink flowers of *Cyclamen coum* unfurl right in the middle of winter; different species of snowdrop appear any time from early winter through to spring and there is always a crocus or two to be found in bloom in the depths of winter, provided the weather is not too frosty. Bright blue blooms of *Iris histrioides* 'Major' as well as those of some of the cultivars of the daintier *I. reticulata*, such as 'Cantab' or 'Harmony', appear surprisingly early in the year.

Routine maintenance

● Trim back old seedheads and dead flowering stems, fern fronds and growths of herbaceous alpines which die down to ground level each year.
● Remove any fallen leaves or other loose herbage from around plants, especially from choice and cushion alpines which may suffer if

The depth of winter provides little colour but a light covering of frost enlivens lichens and foliage on the rock garden.

they are left covered for any length of time. Leaves may also harbour slugs and other pests.
● Check vigorous spreading and mat-forming alpines to see which are encroaching on less sturdy neighbours and trim back as necessary.
● Replenish the top-dressing of rock chippings where patches have appeared on the surface; work the chippings in well around and underneath cushion alpines – this will help keep the collar of the plant drier and less prone to collar-rot.

More serious winter work

● Take advantage of mild weather to construct, reconstruct, repair or improve parts of the rock or scree garden and prepare the area for planting in the spring.

Protecting plants

● At the onset of cold, wet weather, protect cushion-forming and soft, hairy alpines that are prone to winter rot by covering them with a shield of glass or plastic, keeping the sides well ventilated. Secure these well enough to withstand being blown away by winter gales (see page 26).
● Protect the emerging young shoots of bulbs and other plants from slugs and snails by using proprietary slug baits or traps. Always follow the manufacturer's instructions – some baits will harm pets if eaten by them, or poison fish in ponds or, even worse, the beneficial natural fauna of the garden such as toads and hedgehogs.
● Hungry birds can cause considerable damage at this time of year as they search for food. Damage varies from garden to garden and also from season to season but if it is a problem in yours, protect alpines, especially some of the softer cushions, by placing wire mesh or netting over them.
● Check newly planted alpines, especially those in tufa or rock crevices, after a heavy frost. Gently firm back into place any that have been loosened or pushed out.
● A heavy snowfall is unlikely to damage most alpines, indeed it will help to protect them from severe frost or desiccating winds. However, some conifers and shrubs may be at risk. Knock or shake off any snow that weighs them down or threatens to distort or damage branches.

Propagation

● Sow seeds of alpines in scrupulously clean pots using a suitable sterilized, seed compost (see page 29). After sowing, top off the pot with a fine layer of compost and add a protective top-dressing of grit, sharp sand or fine rock chippings. Water well and place in a cool, moist position outdoors – a sand plunge is ideal. Once germination takes place, remove the pots to a cold frame for the rest of the winter. Seed is best sown as early on in winter as possible.

Spring

This is the season most eagerly awaited by alpine gardeners. Immediately the first warm days arrive at the end of winter, alpines start into growth, often coming into flower in just a few days. It is a colourful time of the year with plenty of variety. The successful completion of winter tasks will have ensured that rock and scree gardens and other elements are all at their best for the spring display. Now is the best time to see the results of the previous season's work and to judge the success, or otherwise, of new planting schemes and plant associations. Those that simply do not work, for whatever reason, should be noted for later replanning.

Among the many delights in bloom at this busy season are bright blue spring gentians (*Gentiana verna*), mauve, pink or red forms of *Primula marginata*, white, blue, purple, red or yellow pasque flowers (*Pulsatilla*), the common white or pink arabis, bright aubrietas in many hues, an assortment of tufted and cushion-forming saxifrages and yellow *Draba aizoides*. Adding to the tapestry of spring colours are a host of dwarf bulbs, including: fiery red *Tulipa linifolia*, the more subtle buff and yellow flowers of *T. batalinii* 'Bronze Charm', the delightful chequered bells of *Fritillaria meleagris*, bright blue patches of *Pseudomuscari azureum* (syn. *Muscari azureum*), bright magenta *Cyclamen repandum* with delicately twisted petals, star-shaped blue and white *Chionodoxa gigantea* and the tiny, bright yellow trumpet daffodil *Narcissus asturiensis*.

Routine maintenance

• Remove protective covers of glass or plastic once plants start into active growth.
• Continue to replenish top-dressings of rock chippings if necessary. For established rock gardens a general feed such as a slow-release, low nitrogen fertilizer or bonemeal can be

Aubrieta, *snakeshead fritillarias* (Fritillaria meleagris) *and primroses* (Primula vulgaris) *bring colour to the spring garden.*

added to the top-dressing and thoroughly mixed in. This is highly beneficial and will save a separate operation.
• Dig up any alpines that have succumbed during the winter months, making sure you remove as many roots as possible. Then dig the area over and revitalize the soil with a dressing of bonemeal or similar slow-release fertilizer. Always follow the manufacturer's instructions when using fertilizer.
• Cut away old fronds of winter evergreen ferns such as hart's tongue fern.
• Trim back aubrietas, arabis and similar plants after flowering to encourage compact and strong new growth for flowering the following year.
• Keep a watch for late frosts which can damage emerging shoots or buds of plants like *Meconopsis* and dwarf rhododendrons and protect overnight if necessary.
• Dead-head bulbs if required, except those wanted for seed later in the year, removing

any dying or yellowing leaves, such as those of colchicums, at the same time.
• Remove any dead or diseased growth on dwarf shrubs, especially winter die-back; severe pruning is unnecessary, especially of slow-growing shrubs. Carefully remove any dead patches or leaf rosettes from cushion alpines as these may become sites of infection that will spread to other parts of the plant – use tweezers if necessary.

Planting and propagation

• Spring is one of the best times to plant alpines, whether to replace dead or old, tired specimens or to plant up a new rock garden or scree. Ensure new plants are healthy and weed-free and protect small ones from birds, which can often inadvertently dig them up, by covering them with wire mesh until they are established.
• Ensure that recently planted alpines receive ample moisture, especially during dry, windy weather. Watering should be done carefully and slowly so that the plants are not dislodged or damaged – use a fine sprinkler.
• Vigorous herbaceous types can be divided (see page 31) and replanted in early spring as growth commences. Spare pieces can be planted elsewhere or given to friends.
• Check pots of seeds sown in winter to see which have germinated. Protect seedlings from the depredations of slugs and snails. Prick out most seedlings as soon as they are large enough to handle. Ensure that ungerminated seeds and seedlings are kept sufficiently moist at all times.

Major tasks

• Young, new growth of cushion alpines and seedlings may be scorched by strong, bright spring sunshine. Apply some shading to the alpine house and frame to reduce the effect of the sun's rays.

Summer

The height of the growing season in the alpine garden generally coincides with the driest time of the year. By now the fresh colours of spring have faded to be replaced by strong summer colours. The various pinks (*Dianthus*) provide whites, pinks and reds, the narrow-leaved mats of the rock phloxes bear copious blooms in bright pinks, purples, mauves and reds, while the dwarfer penstemons have attractive tubular flowers in a similar range of colours.

This is the time of year when the Mediterranean element in the alpine garden comes into its own, with aromatic herbs such as thymes, marjorams and lavenders providing much interest and delicious scents. Ornamental onions like yellow *Allium flavum* and pink *A. senescens* flower in mid-summer, their blooms, like those of the aromatic herbs, much visited by butterflies and bees which make the rock garden and scree bed a bustle of pleasant-sounding activity. This is also the main season for the coarser alpines like the prickly, yet majestic, carline thistles (*Carlina acaulis*) and the huge yellow flowers of *Oenothera missouriensis*, which open, like other evening primroses, during the late afternoon.

Summer also sees many spring-flowering alpines coming into fruit. Fruits provide additional interest in the alpine garden in form and colour, as well as giving a bountiful supply of seed. The fruits of prolific seeders such as poppies should be removed, however, before they have a chance to shed their progeny at the expense of more choice alpines.

Although most of the spring-flowering alpines have already gone to seed by this time, interest can be maintained throughout the long summer season by the many delightful forms of cushion, tuft and mat alpines that are eye-catching even after they have finished flowering.

Anemone magellanica *produces a succession of bloom in early summer, followed by fluffy seed heads.*

Routine maintenance

- Tidy up spring-flowering plants. Remove seedheads that are not required, the yellowing leaves of bulbs and any diseased growth.
- Clip back rock roses (*Helianthemum* species and cultivars) after flowering to encourage them to produce strong new shoots for flowering the following year.
- Watch out for pests and diseases, spraying or treating as necessary. Ants often nest under cushion alpines and can quickly destroy a fine plant. Badly damaged plants are best replaced once the offending ants have been removed. Use a proprietary ant powder, following the manufacturer's instructions. Alternatively, pour boiling water directly on to the ants taking great care to avoid any plants.

Watering

- Water regularly and thoroughly during hot, dry spells. A fine mist sprinkler is ideal as it will not damage or flatten precious plants. Watch troughs and other containers carefully, never allowing them to become too dry, otherwise some of the plants will suffer, or even die, if neglected. Remember that they dry out far more rapidly than either a rock garden or scree and should be watered with a watering can.

Planting and propagation

- Start collecting seed from desirable plants, placing it in clearly labelled packets. Keep in a cool, dry place until required.
- Check young, seed-raised plants in frames to ensure they have plenty of moisture and are free of weeds and pests. Keep the frame open and well aerated. The more vigorous young plants can be planted out by mid-summer, allowing them plenty of time to settle in before winter arrives.
- Alpines can still be planted but require regular watering until they show obvious signs of having settled in. This is usually indicated by renewed growth.
- Summer is an important time for taking cuttings; softwood and semi-ripe cuttings of herbaceous and shrubby alpines and rosette cuttings of cushion alpines can be taken now to increase stock or replenish old and tired specimens (see page 30).

Major tasks

- When time permits, this is an excellent period to check the labelling of plants. Ensure that existing labels have not become illegible or, worse, moved in front of the wrong plant. Replace any missing ones. Grey metal labels are long-lasting, legible for many seasons and less obtrusive than other types. White plastic labels can be offensive to the eye and as they quickly become brittle out-of-doors will need to be replaced regularly.
- Increase shading on the alpine house and frames during long, hot, dry spells.

Autumn

Autumn can seem to be the time of year when everything in the alpine garden becomes dormant. This is not the case, though, as there is still so much to interest and excite the eye. Many summer flowers last well into autumn, adding colour until the frosts arrive, but there are also lots of new excitements coming into bloom at this time. The brilliant blue flowers of the autumn gentians, particularly *Gentiana sino-ornata*, *G.* × *macaulayi* and *G.* × *stevenagensis*, are an arresting sight, especially when planted in drifts. Autumn bulbs put on a fine show: white and pink *Cyclamen hederifolium* and *C. cilicium*, together with autumn-flowering crocuses such as mauve or white *C. goulimyi* and the sturdier white or pale lilac of *C. niveus*, are the finest at this time of year. Bright yellow is provided by the bold crocus-like flowers of *Sternbergia lutea* and *S. sicula* which like all the heat and sun they can get and as little disturbance as possible. There is even a snowdrop, *Galanthus reginae-olgae*, that flowers at this time of year, just before its leaves appear, making it a novelty well worth seeking out.

Autumn fruits add additional interest to the alpine garden, in particular the red berries of the dwarf rowan (*Sorbus reducta*) and the white, pink, orange or red berries of the prickly, acid-loving pernettyas.

Autumn is also a time for reviewing the alpine garden and noting the successes and failures of the year. Plans to improve areas that you are not happy with can be formulated now. Prepare the way, perhaps, for large reconstruction jobs, such as changing the shape of the rock garden, and other manual work which is best carried out, as weather permits, through the winter months. Careful planning in autumn will enable you to approach the work in less of a rush as winter and spring approaches and ultimately lead to much better results.

The striking blue berries of Gaultheria trichophylla *are produced from late summer through to autumn.*

Routine maintenance

● Dead-head all prolific seeders, for instance poppies and ornamental onions, before they have a chance to cast their seed around at the expense of other alpines. This will save a good deal of weeding in the following season.

● Remove fallen leaves and any dead plants that have accumulated around the rocks and in the crevices on the rock garden as these can harbour slugs and other pests.

● Clear away excessive growth of trailing and mat-forming alpines from areas where autumn- and winter-flowering bulbs are known to be planted.

● Remove moss and liverworts from rocks and tufa where they are likely to encroach on choice alpines; mosses and liverworts tend to go on growing through the winter and can become a menace by the spring.

● Check that cushion alpines in particular have a good collar of rock chippings around them. This will help keep the necks of plants

relatively dry during the winter months when little moisture is required.

Planting and propagation

● Guard young and newly established plants from slugs and snails, which are particularly active at this time of year.

● Autumn is the most important season for collecting seed. Collect seed of choice and rare plants, marking each packet with details of name and origin, if these are known. Excess seed can be sent to seed exchanges of alpine plant societies or horticultural clubs and organizations.

● Commence seed sowing, using fresh seed for species that lose viability rapidly or germinate more erratically once dried, such as cyclamen or primulas.

● Take hardwood cuttings of dwarf shrubs where appropriate.

● Many robust herbaceous alpines like the bugles (*Ajuga*), skullcaps (*Scutellaria*), *Primula vulgaris* and *Viola cornuta* can be lifted and divided now without fear of harming the plants in any way.

● Planting can continue in the early autumn and, provided the weather remains mild, there is still plenty of time for alpines to settle in before the onset of winter. This is a good time to plant conifers, but they should be well watered in and checked regularly during dry spells.

Major tasks

● Net over any pools on the rock garden to prevent leaves and other debris from clogging or fouling the water. A healthy, well-planted pool will attract a variety of wild life into the garden.

● Clean pots in preparation for seed-sowing or for repotting alpines.

● Remove shading from the alpine house and frames.

KEY PLANTS

The alpine plants featured in this chapter are very much a personal choice, although I have tried to present a full and varied range of plants that are currently available. They are described together with details of their preferred growing conditions to enable you to make your own selections.

Anemone blanda *'Atrocaerulea', one of the earliest spring bulbs, is an easy and very accommodating plant, spreading freely in most gardens. The striking purplish-blue flowers open in bright sunshine but remain closed on dull, rainy days.*

Choosing alpines can provide hours of pleasure as you search through books, manuals and illustrated catalogues. At first, though, the choice of available plants seems enormous and daunting. Before making any purchase, it is a good idea to familiarize yourself with those alpines that do particularly well in your area. Visit gardens and consult your local nurseries to see which plants they grow successfully. Until you have had some practical experience of these fascinating little plants, avoid any that are clearly tricky to maintain – an honest nurseryman will be only too keen to advise you.

Your prime considerations when working with alpines will often be quite different from those required in other parts of the flower garden. When planting, you will need some care and foresight. Many alpines are discrete little plants that need space and light around them and do not take kindly to crowding. It is easy to overcrowd them because they are so small initially and so it is especially important to ascertain the likely ultimate size of each plant before deciding where to position it.

Once you are familiar with the basic requirements, you can have great fun planning combinations of sizes and shapes. Consider which alpines would be effective sandwiched between two adjacent rocks or crammed into a crevice, which would look best cascading over the edge of a wall, or which would look attractive amidst rock fragments. Many alpines have very brightly coloured flowers which appear as jewels when set against a background of rocks or rock chippings.

The rock garden, scree, raised bed and trough provide the various habitats for your alpine plants to thrive in, but they should also be attractive in their own right. Aim for a happy balance between plants and rocks and resist covering the whole area in a mass of plants. Not only would this be difficult to maintain but it would be contrary to the way many alpines grow naturally.

Most alpine plants are fully hardy as far as temperature is concerned, that is they are able to withstand the cold temperatures of a continental winter. Those that are not fully hardy are indicated as frost-hardy to −5°C (23°F), or half-hardy and require protection from winter frosts. A number of alpines that are temperature-hardy will not tolerate much moisture in winter and will rot away in damp or moist conditions. Placing a piece of glass or similar covering above them keeps the rain off while allowing the free movement of air around them.

Perennials

Aethionema

The delightful plants in this genus are either perennials or small evergreen subshrubs. They are easy to propagate from softwood cuttings or from seed. Persian stone cress, *A. grandiflorum*, has bluish-green leaves and lax racemes of rose-pink flowers from late spring to mid-summer. *A. pulchellum* is similar with bright pink flowers.
Size H: 30cm/1ft; S: 25cm/10in. **Aspect** Sun. **Hardiness** Fully hardy. **Soil** Any, well-drained.
Other species A. 'Warley Rose': to 15cm (6in) high, with a profusion of deep pink flowers in summer.

Alpine bells see *Soldanella*

Alpine catchfly see *Lychnis alpina*

Alyssum

Clump- or carpet-forming plants with evergreen leaves and yellow flowers. Yellow alyssum or gold dust, *A. saxatile*, is one of the largest species with attractive oval, grey-green leaves and sprays of small flowers from mid-spring to mid-summer. 'Citrina', pale cream-yellow flowers; 'Variegatum', yellow flowers, cream-edged leaves.
Size H: 20cm/8in; S: 30cm/1ft. **Aspect** Sun. **Hardiness** Fully hardy. **Soil** Any, well-drained.

Androsace
(Rock jasmines)
These plants form dense, tight cushions, spreading mats or leafy rosettes, with solitary or clustered flowers. *A.*

lanuginosa is one of the best for the rock garden, making mats of silky, grey leaf rosettes. The soft lilac-pink flowers are borne in rounded heads on a common stalk from late spring to the beginning of summer.
Size H: 4cm/1½in; S: 20cm/8in. **Aspect** Sun. **Hardiness** Fully hardy. **Soil** Any, well-drained.
Other species A. *sarmentosa*: resembles *A. lanuginosa*, with open rosettes and bright pink flowers.

Anemone
(Windflowers)
Rhizomatous plants with large, bright flowers immediately above a whorl of leaves. *A. blanda* bears flowers 4–5cm (1½–2in) across, each one with up to 14 narrow, blue petals, borne from the end of winter until the end of spring. Good cultivars include: 'Atrocaerulea', intense blue flowers; 'Radar', white-centred, pinkish-red flowers; 'White Splendour', glistening white flowers.
Size H: 5–10cm/2–4in; S: 5–15cm/2–6in. **Aspect** Sun or part-shade. **Hardiness** Fully hardy. **Soil** Any.
Other species A. *magellanica*: tufted, to 20cm (8in) high, with several cream-white flowers on a common stalk in late spring and early summer.

Aquilegia
(Columbines)
These are short-lived perennials with cut foliage, many leaflets and spurred flowers. Only the smaller types are suitable for the alpine garden. *A. flabellata* has bluish-green leaves and bluish-mauve flowers with white-

tipped petals. The dwarf form 'Nana' is the best. All flower from early to mid-summer.
Size H: 10–25cm/4–10in; S: 8–12cm/3–4¾in. **Aspect** Full sun. **Hardiness** Fully hardy. **Soil** Any, well-drained.

Arabis
(Rock cresses)
Vigorous, mat-forming plants with rather coarse rosettes of toothed leaves and racemes of four-petalled flowers. *A. caucasica* bears its white or pale pink flowers from early spring to early summer. Good cultivars include: 'Flore Pleno', double, white; 'Variegata', white, cream-edged leaves. The form *rosea* has rose-pink flowers; *A.* × *arendsii* 'Rosabella' deep pink flowers.
Size H: 8–15cm/3–6in; S: 30cm/1ft. **Aspect** Full sun. **Hardiness** Fully hardy. **Soil** Any, well-drained.

Armeria
(Thrifts)
Cushion-forming plants with heads of small flowers borne on leafless stalks. *A. maritima* has grass-like leaves and white to pink flowers from late spring to mid-summer. Good cultivars include: 'Birch Pink', rose-pink; 'Laucheana', bright red; 'Merlin', rich pink; 'Vindictive', reddish-pink.
Size H: 8–12cm/3–4¾in; S: 10–20cm/4–8in. **Aspect** Full sun. **Hardiness** Fully hardy. **Soil** Any, well-drained.
Other species *A. juniperifolia*: denser cushions of greyish, pointed leaves and short-stalked pink flowers.

Asperula suberosa
Forming lax mats or cushions of soft, downy, grey leaves, *A. suberosa* is a gem with masses of pale pink, four-lobed flowers in early and mid-summer.
Size H: 4–8cm/1½–3in; S: 10–25cm/4–10in. **Aspect** Full sun. **Hardiness** Fully hardy. **Soil** Any, well-drained.

Aubrieta
The various forms of this favourite are all derived from *A. deltoidea* which forms dense, evergreen mats made up of grey-green leaf rosettes. Short racemes of vivid mauve, purple, pink, red or white flowers in spring.
Size H: 8–20cm/3–8in; S: 30–60cm/1–2ft. **Aspect** Sun. **Hardiness** Fully hardy. **Soil** Any, well-drained.

Balloon flower
see *Platycodon grandiflorus*

Bellflowers see *Campanula*

Bistorts see *Polygonum*

Blue poppies see *Meconopsis*

Campanula
(Bellflowers)
There are many small alpine bellflowers that are ideal for the rock garden and troughs. Fairy's thimble, *C. cochleariifolia*, is quite charming although it can be invasive. The low, leafy stems carry little, nodding blue bells from late spring to mid-summer. 'Alba' is a white form and 'Flore Pleno'

Androsace sarmentosa

Perennials form the hub of the alpine garden, providing mats, tufts, discrete rosettes and cushions of varied, exciting forms. Many are very colourful, catching the eye with their brash blooms.

has double, lavender-blue flowers.
Size H: 6–9cm/2¼–3½in; S: 20cm/8in or more. **Aspect** Full sun. **Hardiness** Fully hardy. **Soil** Any, well-drained.
Other species All flower between mid-summer and early autumn. *C. carpatica*: clump-forming with large, erect, purple-blue or white bells. *C. portenschlagiana*: vigorous, forming dense tufts with violet-blue flowers.

Campions, catchflies see *Silene*

*Cyclamen
hederifolium*

Celmisia

Genus of plants from New Zealand with white, daisy-like flowers. *C. coriacea* has handsome, evergreen, silvery rosettes of large, sword-shaped leaves and big flowers during early and mid-summer.
Size H: 20–35cm/8–14in; S: 30cm/1ft. **Aspect** Full sun. **Hardiness** Frost-hardy. **Soil** Well-drained, humus-rich, acid.

Chiastophyllum oppositifolium

Tufted succulent with paired leaves, mostly arranged in lax, basal rosettes. Thick stems support elegant, catkin-like, arched racemes of tiny, bright yellow flowers throughout summer.
Size H: 15–20cm/6–8in; S: 10–20cm/4–8in. **Aspect** Sun or shade. **Hardiness** Fully hardy. **Soil** Any, well-drained.

Chrysanthemopsis hosmariense
syn. *Leucanthemum hosmariense*

A vigorous, grey-green, hummocky plant with neatly dissected foliage and large, white, daisy flowers from late spring to mid-summer.
Size H and S: 30–60cm/1–2ft. **Aspect** Sun. **Hardiness** Frost-hardy. **Soil** Light, well-drained.

Columbines see *Aquilegia*

Corydalis

Easy to grow and with rather ferny foliage, these somewhat succulent perennials are deservedly popular. The genus includes both tuberous-rooted and fibrous-rooted species.

Tuberous-rooted species:
C. solida has solid tubers, several stem leaves and a single raceme of pale to deep pink or purple flowers. 'George P Baker' has deep rose-red flowers.
Size H: 8–15cm/3–6in; S: 10–20cm/4–8in. **Aspect** Sun or part-shade. **Hardiness** Fully hardy. **Soil** Moist, humus-rich.

Fibrous-rooted species:
C. lutea forms mounds of soft green foliage speckled with yellow flowers for most of the year. It seeds freely.
Size H: 15–20cm/6–8in; S: 15–30cm/6–12in. **Aspect** Part-shade. **Hardiness** Fully hardy. **Soil** Any.
Other species *C. flexuosa*: splendid, soft, ferny leaves and masses of sky-blue flowers of great charm.

Cranesbills see *Geranium*

Creeping bluet
see *Hedyotis michauxii*

Cyclamen
(Sowbreads)

Several of these ever-popular, little, tuberous-rooted plants are easy to grow in the average garden. *C. hederifolium* has attractively variegated, ivy-like leaves and numerous pink flowers in late summer and autumn. The form *album* has pure white flowers.
Size H: 8–15cm/3–6in; S: 15–30cm/6–12in. **Aspect** Sun or part-shade. **Hardiness** Fully hardy. **Soil** Leafy, well-drained loam.
Other species *C. coum*: rounded or kidney-shaped, plain or variegated leaves and smaller, dumpier flowers from pale to deep magenta-pink or white, in winter and early spring. *C. repandum*: variegated, ivy-like leaves and carmine-magenta flowers in spring; requires a sheltered spot.

Devil's claw see *Physoplexis comosa*

Dianthus
(Pinks)

A large and complicated genus with many plants suitable for the rock garden, troughs and similar containers. *D. alpinus* forms flat cushions of dark green, oblong leaves, which are covered with large solitary, pink or purplish flowers all summer long. 'Joan's Blood' has red flowers and bronzed leaves.

Size H: 6–10cm/2¼–4in; S: 6–20cm/ 2¼–8in. **Aspect** Sun. **Hardiness** Fully hardy. **Soil** Well-drained, gritty and calcareous.

Other species *D. petraeus*: spiky, greyish cushions and fragrant, white flowers with fringed petals. *D. deltoides*: the maiden pink; mats of trailing stems bearing small, white, pink or reddish flowers; often seeds freely. *D. erinaceus*: prickly hedgehog cushions to 50cm (20in) bearing small, solitary or paired, pink flowers. They are also many colourful named cultivars available.

Draba
(Whitlow grasses)

Tufted or cushion-forming alpines with small, yellow flowers in clusters or racemes. *D. aizoides* has small rosettes of bristle-edged leaves and lemon-yellow flowers in mid- and late spring.

Size H: 5–15cm/2–6in; S: 8–20cm/ 3–8in. **Aspect** Sun. **Hardiness** Fully hardy. **Soil** Well-drained.

Dragonmouth
see *Horminum pyrenaicum*

Edelweiss
see *Leontopodium alpinum*

Erinus alpinus
(Fairy foxglove)

Ideal for rock gardens, troughs or dry walls, this charming little alpine has evergreen leaf rosettes and small racemes of white, pink or rose-purple

flowers from late spring to mid-summer. Although short-lived, established plants will usually seed around. Size H and S: 5–8cm/2–3in. **Aspect** Sun. **Hardiness** Fully hardy. **Soil** Any well-drained soil.

Erodium
(Stork's bills)

Closely related to geraniums, plants in this genus have lobed or dissected foliage and attractive flowers, often with the upper two petals blotched. *E. petraeum* forms greyish-green tussocks and bears saucer-shaped, pink flowers veined with red throughout summer. Size H: 15–20cm/6–8in; S: 15–25cm/ 6–10in. **Aspect** Sun. **Hardiness** Frost-hardy. **Soil** Well-drained.
Other species *E. reichardii* (syn. *E. chamaedrioides*): one of the best forms; produces tight cushions of small, oakshaped leaves, studded with solitary white or pink flowers.

Evening primroses see *Oenothera*

Fairy foxglove see *Erinus alpinus*

Flaxes see *Linum*

Gentiana
(Gentians)

Often bearing vivid blue flowers, this genus is one of the most popular groups for the alpine garden. Many plants are tricky and demanding to grow but some of the loveliest are quite easy. The well-known trumpet gentian of the Alps, *G. acaulis* (syn.

G. kochiana), forms mats of leathery, deep green leaves beset with large, intense deep blue, trumpet-shaped flowers from mid- to late-spring. Size H: 3–8cm/1¼–3in; S: 10–30cm/ 4–12in. **Aspect** Sun. **Hardiness** Fully hardy. **Soil** Well-drained, calcareous to neutral.
Other species *G. septemfida*: coarser than the others, forming tufts, with large oval leaves and stems bearing a cluster of deep blue, bell-shaped flowers in mid- and late summer. *G. sino-ornata*: trailing stems, freshgreen, linear leaves and large, royalblue, trumpet-shaped flowers in early and mid-autumn; another gem but requires peaty, acid soil.

Erinus alpinus

Geranium
(Cranesbills)

Only the smaller species of this large and colourful group are suitable for the rock garden. *G. dalmaticum* forms spreading clumps of rounded, lobed, rather shiny leaves. The deep pink flowers are borne in clusters during late spring and early summer. 'Album' has white flowers.
Size H: 8–12cm/3–4¾in; S: 20–40cm/8–16in. **Aspect** Sun or part-shade. **Hardiness** Fully hardy. **Soil** Any, well-drained.
Other species *G. cinereum*: hummock-forming with pale lilac-pink flowers with deeper veins in early and mid-

Hacquetia epipactis

summer; subsp. *subcaulescens*, intense magenta-red flowers; 'Ballerina', purple-centred lilac flowers.

Gypsophila

The alpine gypsophila, *G. repens*, has slender, prostrate stems with paired green or bronze leaves and small, white or pale to rose-pink flowers in summer. 'Rosea' has mid-pink flowers; 'Rosea Plena', double, pink.
Size H: 3–6cm/1¼–2¼in; S: 20–40cm/8–16in. **Aspect** Sun. **Hardiness** Fully hardy. **Soil** Any, well-drained.

Hacquetia epipactis

A small leafy plant with glossy, three-lobed leaves. The golden-yellow flowers appear close to the ground from late winter through spring and are most noted for the ruff of shiny, yellowish-green bracts that surround the flower clusters.
Size H: 15–25cm/6–10in; S: 15–30cm/6–12in. **Aspect** Sun or part-shade. **Hardiness** Fully hardy. **Soil** Moist, leafy.

Hedyotis michauxii
syn. *Houstonia caerulea*
(Creeping bluet)

A creeping, mat-forming plant with tiny, bright green leaves and many star-shaped, china-blue flowers from mid-summer to early autumn.
Size H: 3–6cm/1¼–2¼in; S: 10–30cm/4–12in. **Aspect** Full or part-shade. **Hardiness** Fully hardy. **Soil** Moist.

Horminum pyrenaicum
(Dragonmouth)

A tufted perennial with basal rosettes of oval, scallop-margined, shiny, deep green leaves. It bears spikes of deep violet-blue, occasionally white, two-lipped flowers throughout summer.
Size H: 15–20cm/6–8in; S: 15–30cm/6–12in. **Aspect** Sun or part-shade. **Hardiness** Fully hardy. **Soil** Any, well-drained.

Houseleeks see *Sempervivum*

Incarvillea mairei

Forming a tuft of basal, somewhat lobed, dark green leaves, this rather exotic-looking plant bears large, trumpet-shaped flowers of rich pink-purple on a stout stem in early to mid-summer. The cultivar 'Frank Ludlow' has deep pink flowers.
Size H and S: 20–30cm/8–12in. **Aspect** Sun. **Hardiness** Fully hardy but crowns may need a protective mulch in winter. **Soil** Any, well-drained.

Leontopodium alpinum
(Edelweiss)

A tufted plant with narrow, grey-green leaves and head of insignificant flowers surrounded by a ruff of furry, white bracts. 'Mignon' is a neater plant and has narrower bracts. Dwarfer and with very large white bracts, *L. nivale* is superior but rather scarce.
Size H: 5–15cm/2–6in; S: 8–15cm/3–6in. **Aspect** Sun. **Hardiness** Fully hardy. **Soil** Any, well-drained.

Linum
(Flaxes)

The satiny flowers of this group of colourful, narrow-leaved and rather wiry-stemmed plants open only in sunny weather. *L. arboreum* forms evergreen tussocks, woody at the base, with deep blue-green, elliptical leaves. The terminal clusters of bright yellow flowers appear in late spring.
Size H and S: 20–30cm/8–12in. **Aspect** Sun. **Hardiness** Frost-hardy. **Soil** Well-drained, alkaline.
Other species *L. suffruticosum* subsp. *salsoloides* 'Nanum': tufted, greyish plant with needle-like leaves and white flowers centred and veined with pink or violet; 10–15cm/4–6in high.

Lychnis alpina
(Alpine catchfly)

Somewhat sticky, this small, tufted plant has narrow, untoothed, dark green leaves and terminal clusters of pinkish-purple flowers from the end of spring to mid-summer. It is short-lived but often seeds around freely.
Size H: 5–15cm/2–6in; S: 10–15cm/4–6in. **Aspect** Sun. **Hardiness** Fully hardy. **Soil** Any, well-drained.

Meconopsis
(Blue poppies)

Only the smaller plants in this genus of perennials are suitable for the alpine garden. The welsh poppy, *M. cambrica*, forms erect, bright green tufts with yellow or orange, poppy-like flowers borne on slender stalks from late spring through to early autumn. It seeds freely and can be invasive.

Size H: 30–60cm/1–2ft; S: 20–40cm/8–16in. **Aspect** Sun or part-shade. **Hardiness** Fully hardy. **Soil** Moist.
Other species *M. horridula*: bristly leaf rosettes and stems with blue or lilac-blue, poppy-like flowers; dies after flowering; needs a moist, peaty soil. *M. quintuplinervia*: spreading plant with pale lavender, bell flowers from late spring to mid-summer; needs a moist, peaty soil.

Milkworts see *Polygala*

Oenothera
(Evening primroses)

O. missouriensis is a tufted plant with spreading stems and oval, deep green leaves. The large yellow flowers open widely in the evening in summer.
Size H: 8–12cm/3–4¾in; S: 20–40cm/8–16in. **Aspect** Sun. **Hardiness** Fully hardy. **Soil** Well-drained, gritty.
Other species *O. caespitosa*: fragrant, white flowers which turn pink.

Pansies see *Viola*

Papaver
(Poppies)

Only the small alpine types of this popular genus are suitable for the rock garden. Plants in the *P. alpinum* group (including *P. burseri* and *P. rhaeticum*) are small tufted, short-lived perennials often grown as annuals. The grey-green leaves are finely dissected. The long-stalked, solitary flowers, which

appear from late spring to early autumn, are white, yellow or orange.
Size H: 10–20cm/4–8in; S: 10–15cm/4–6in. **Aspect** Sun. **Hardiness** Fully hardy. **Soil** Well-drained, gritty, neutral to alkaline.
Other species *P. miyabeanum*: dwarfer with hairy, soft grey leaves and smaller, pale yellow flowers.

Oenothera missouriensis

Pasque flowers see *Pulsatilla*

Penstemon

A North American genus of large herbaceous types and charming little alpines with racemes of two-lipped, tubular flowers. Mountain pride, *P. newberryi*, makes evergreen mats of leathery, dull green leaves with bright rose-pink flowers in mid-summer.
Size H: 10–20cm/4–8in; S: 20–30cm/8–12in. **Aspect** Sun. **Hardiness** Frost-hardy. **Soil** Gritty, well-drained.

Platycodon grandiflorus var. *mariesii*

Phlox

Salver-shaped flowers which are borne in clusters or racemes are characteristic of this North American genus of large herbaceous and smaller alpine species. The numerous small, needle-like leaves of *P. subulata* make evergreen mats or mounds which are studded with white, pink, mauve or crimson flowers from late spring through to mid-summer.
Size H: 4–10cm/1½–4in; S: 8–30cm/3–12in. **Aspect** Sun. **Hardiness** Fully hardy. **Soil** Gritty, well-drained.
Other species *P. adsurgens*: mat-forming with oval leaves and upright stems, bearing white, pink or purple flowers with broad, overlapping petals; requires acid, peaty soil; 'Wagon Wheel', pink with narrow petals. *P. douglasii*: attractive mounds of narrow leaves with full-petalled, mauve, purple or crimson flowers. *P.* 'Chattahoochee': lax, somewhat spreading habit with narrow leaves and red-eyed lavender flowers; frost-hardy.

Physoplexis comosa
syn. *Phyteuma comosum*
(Devil's claw)

Devil's claw is an extraordinary and sought-after plant. The basal rosettes of rather fleshy, coarsely toothed leaves bear low clusters of lantern-shaped, pinkish-lilac flowers, their petals tipped with blackish-violet, in summer. They dislike winter wet and are prone to attack from slugs.
Size H: 4–8cm/1½–3in; S: 6–12cm/2¼–4¾in. **Aspect** Sun. **Hardiness** Fully hardy. **Soil** Gritty, calcareous.

Pinks see *Dianthus*

Platycodon grandiflorus
(Balloon flower)

A stiff-stemmed plant with broad, oval, bluish-green leaves. The large blue or purplish-blue, bell-shaped flowers, with five triangular lobes, open from swollen, balloon-shaped buds in early summer. The purplish-blue flowered *P. grandiflorus* 'Apoyama', which grows to only 13cm (5in), and *P. grandiflorus* var. *mariesii*, with purplish-blue flowers, are the best dwarf forms for the rock garden.
Size H: 10–30cm/4–12in; S: 15–30cm/6–12in. **Aspect** Sun. **Hardiness** Fully hardy. **Soil** Any, well-drained.

Polygala
(Milkworts)

With small, winged and lipped flowers and untoothed leaves, the milkworts are a charming little group

of perennials or subshrubs. *P. calcarea* makes lax rosettes of spoon-shaped leaves from which arise leafy stems with dense racemes of deep blue flowers from late spring to mid-summer. Good cultivars are: 'Bulley's Variety', with its prostrate habit, and 'Lillet', a fine compact form.
Size H: 2–8cm/¾–3in; S: 8–20cm/3–8in. **Aspect** Sun. **Hardiness** Fully hardy. **Soil** Well-drained, gritty, alkaline to neutral.

Polygonum
(Bistorts)

The carpeting or trailing habits of these narrow-leaved plants make them particularly effective for draping over a large rock in the garden. Erect stems carry spikes of small flowers. Carpet-forming *P. affine* has oblong, leathery, deep green leaves that often turn a bronze colour during autumn. The oblong flower-spikes are pink or rose-red, from late-summer to early autumn. 'Darjeeling Red', deep red flowers; 'Donald Lowndes', deep rose-red.
Size H: 15–22cm/6–8½in; S: 20–50cm/8–20in. **Aspect** Sun or part-shade. **Hardiness** Fully hardy. **Soil** Any, moist.

Poppies see *Papaver*

Pratia pedunculata
syn. *Lobelia pedunculata*

A rather moss-like, mat-forming, bright green evergreen. It bears numerous solitary, long-stalked, star-shaped, mauve-pink flowers throughout summer and into early autumn. **Size** H: 1–2cm/½–¾in; S: 10–60cm/4in–2ft. **Aspect** Shade. **Hardiness** Frost-hardy. **Soil** Any, moist.

Primula
(Primroses)

Including numerous exciting and colourful species and cultivars, this enormous group is prominent in the alpine garden. In rock gardens that are large enough to include water courses or pools, some of the large bog primulas such as *P. bulleyana*, *P. japonica*, *P. prolifera*, *P. pulverulenta* and *P. sikkimensis* can be grown successfully. For the average-sized rock garden, there is a multitude of smaller, but equally colourful, plants from which to make a choice. These can be divided into several groups for convenience, according to their preferred type of soil.

Group 1. Average, moist but well-drained soil:
The common primrose, *P. vulgaris*, is well known for the solitary soft-yellow flowers borne above clumps of bright green leaf rosettes from the end of winter until mid-spring. Interesting cultivars for the garden include single- and double-flowered forms in yellow, pink, red or blue.
Size H: 10–20cm/4–8in; S: 15–30cm/6–12in. **Aspect** Sun or part-shade. **Hardiness** Fully hardy.

Group 2. Well-drained, gritty, alkaline to neutral soil:
Represented by the auricula, *P. auricula*, these plants form groups of rather fleshy-leaved rosettes, neatly toothed along the margins, sometimes white and mealy over the surface. Umbels of yellow, funnel-shaped flowers with mealy-white centres appear from mid- to late spring. There are many cultivars in a wide range of flower colours. **Size** H: 10–20cm/4–8in; S: 10–30cm/4–12in. **Aspect** Sun or part-shade. **Hardiness** Fully hardy.

Group 3. Moist, gritty, alkaline soil:
The rather thick-leaved rosettes of *P. marginata* have toothed margins edged with yellowish or white mealy farina which sometimes covers the entire surface of the leaves. Small umbels of lavender to bluish-lilac or almost violet flowers appear in mid- and late spring. Among the best cultivars are: 'Beatrice Lascaris', blue; 'Caerulea', blue, strongly mealy leaves; 'Holden Clough', small blue flowers and mealy leaves; 'Prichard's Variety', large, lilac-blue flowers with a white eye. **Size** H: 8–15cm/3–6in; S: 10–30cm/4–12in. **Aspect** Sun. **Hardiness** Fully hardy.

Group 4. Moist soil that does not dry out:
P. rosea forms clumps of deep green, finely toothed leaves that are only partly developed when clusters of carmine-rose flowers are freely borne from mid- to late spring. **Size** H: 8–15cm/3–6in; S: 10–20cm/4–8in. **Aspect** Sun or part-shade. **Hardiness** Fully hardy.
Other species *P. frondosa*: neat clumps of pale, mealy leaves with long-stalked umbels of small, lilac-rose flowers with a pale yellow eye.

Primula sieboldii

Group 5. Moist, peaty, acid, soil:
P. petiolaris forms rather flat rosettes of dark green, toothed leaves in the centre of which sits a posy of yellow-eyed, purplish-pink flowers. **Size** H: 5–10cm/2–4in; S: 8–15cm/3–6in. **Aspect** Sun or part-shade. **Hardiness** Fully hardy.
Other species *P. bhutanica*: similar but with short umbels of cream- or white-eyed, purplish-blue flowers.

Group 6. Moist, peaty soil in shade:
P. polyneura has lax tufts of rounded, hairy, shallowly lobed leaves and one-sided umbels of bright rose-purple flowers in late spring and early summer. **Size** H and S: 20–30cm/8–12in. **Aspect** Part- or full shade. **Hardiness** Fully hardy.
Other species *P. sieboldii*: spreading carpets of lobed, bright pale green leaves, with small umbels of white, pink or purple flowers in late spring and early summer; can be invasive; various named forms are available.

Pterocephalus perennis
syn. *P. parnassii*

This mat-forming plant has soft, crinkly, grey-green leaves just above which solitary, scabious-like, pinkish-lavender flowers nestle in summer.
Size H: 4–6cm/1½–2¼in; S: 10–30cm/4–12in. **Aspect** Sun. **Hardiness** Fully hardy. **Soil** Gritty, well-drained, neutral to alkaline.

Pulsatilla
(Pasque flowers)

Related to the anemones, these clump-forming plants with finely cut, feathery foliage constitute one of the loveliest groups in the alpine garden. Their solitary silky, bell- or cup-shaped flowers appear from mid- to late spring and are followed by handsome, feath-

Pulsatilla rubra

ery fruits. Mature plants hate being moved but new ones are easy to grow from fresh seed. *P. vulgaris* has purple flowers. The form *alba* is white.
Size H: 12–23cm/4¾–9in; S: 15–25cm/6–10in. **Aspect** Sun. **Hardiness** Fully hardy. **Soil** Any, well-drained, neutral or alkaline.
Other species *P. halleri*: pale green foliage and large, upright, lavender-blue, open bells, with double-flowered forms also available. *P. rubra*: like *P. vulgaris*, but with deep red flowers.

Rock cresses see *Arabis*

Rock jasmines see *Androsace*

Rock soapwort
see *Saponaria ocymoides*

Saponaria ocymoides
(Rock soapwort)

Mat-forming with lax, often rather sprawling, stems and small, oval, deep green leaves, this species bears lots of pink flowers from late spring right through summer. The cultivar 'Alba' is white; 'Rubra Compacta' is dwarf.
Size H: 4–10cm/1½–4in; S: 20–40cm/8–16in. **Aspect** Sun. **Hardiness** Fully hardy. **Soil** Dry, well-drained.

Saxifraga
(Saxifrages)

Many species, hybrids and cultivars of this very large and important group are grown by alpine gardeners. Mostly forming tight cushions of numerous small leaf rosettes, they are excellent for the rock garden, raised beds, troughs and as feature plants in blocks of tufa. *S. burseriana* makes small, grey-green cushions of narrow, pointed leaves. Its reddish stems carry solitary white flowers from late winter until the end of spring.
Size H: 3–5cm/1¼–2in; S: 5–10cm/2–4in. **Aspect** Part-shade. **Hardiness** Fully hardy. **Soil** Well-drained, alkaline.
Other species *S. cochlearis*: crowded, lime-encrusted rosettes and light sprays of small, white flowers to 20cm (8in) high. *S. cotyledon*: large, handsome, deep grey-green rosettes, to 12cm (4¾in) across, and large sprays of white flowers throughout summer. *S. grisebachii*: handsome, rather flat, silvery-grey rosettes up to 7cm (2¾in) across, with reddish-purple racemes to 12cm (4¾in) high; 'Wisley', particularly well coloured. *S. longifolia*: large, solitary, lime-encrusted, rosettes of numerous linear leaves, eventually producing a huge, arching panicle of white flowers after which it dies; 'Tumbling Waters', several rosettes and sprays of pure white. *S. oppositifolia*: flat mats of dark green leaves with creeping stems and practically stalkless, pink to purplish-red flowers in late spring and early summer. *S. paniculata*: cushions of lime-encrusted rosettes with 30cm (1ft) or more panicles of white flowers.

Hybrids (a small selection):
S. × anglica: domed cushions and pink or purple flowers in clusters of one to three; 'Beatrix Stanley', red; 'Christine', red to salmon-pink on a silvery

cushion; 'Cranbourne', rose-pink; 'Myra', rose-carmine on a silver-grey cushion; 'Winifred', greyish cushions with dark-centred, deep pink flowers. *S. × apiculata*: large, green cushions with yellow flowers from early to mid-spring; 'Gregor Mendel', pale yellow. *S. × boydii*: spiky, grey cushions with yellow flowers, similar to *S. burseriana*; 'Aretiastrum' ('Valerie Finnis'), fine, free-flowering, pale yellow; 'Hindhead Seedling', taller, pale yellow. *S. × irvingii*: slow-growing, tightly packed, grey cushions and pink flowers; 'Jenkinsiae', pale pink with darker veins; 'Rubella', pale pink or whitish; 'Walter Irving', pale lilac-pink. *S.* 'Southside Seedling', large, handsome plant forming deep green rosettes 10cm (4in) across with tall panicles, up to 35cm (14in), of numerous white flowers blotched with dull crimson.

Sedum
(Stonecrops)

A large genus of succulent plants, the smaller ones ideal for the alpine garden. The star-like flowers each have six to eight petals. Most root readily from stem or leaf cuttings at almost any time of the year. Common stonecrop, *S. acre*, forms bright green mats with spreading shoots and is covered with a mass of bright yellow flowers in early and mid-summer.

Size H: 2–6cm/¾–2¼in; S: 10–30cm/4–12in. **Aspect** Sun. **Hardiness** Fully hardy. **Soil** Gritty, well-drained.

Other species Narrow leaves, round or oval in section: *S. ochroleucum*: vigorous with spreading stems covered in narrow, pointed, greyish or whitish foliage and pale yellow flowers. *S. pulchellum*: close tufts of crowded, narrow, pale green leaves with reddish stems and rose-purple flowers in mid- to late summer.

Broad and flat leaves: *S. cyaneum*: sprawling habit with paired or alternate oblong, lilac-grey leaves and rose-purple flowers from late summer through to mid-autumn. *S. spathulifolium*: brittle stems bearing numerous lax rosettes of spoon-shaped, grey-green, purple or pinkish leaves and flat heads of yellow flowers in mid- to late autumn; widely grown, good for shady spots.

Sempervivum
(Houseleeks)

The houseleeks are a large group of succulent plants with neat, symmetrical, tightly clustered leaf rosettes and stiff clusters of star-shaped flowers. They are easily propagated from detached rosettes. The cobweb houseleek, *S. arachnoideum*, has small rosettes of cobwebbed leaves which form a flat cushion. The reddish or pinkish flowers are borne in summer and into early autumn. 'Minor' is a small version with tight rosettes.

Size H: 6–12cm/2¼–4¾in; S: 5–30cm/2–12in. **Aspect** Sun. **Hardiness** Fully hardy. **Soil** Any, well-drained.

Other species *S. ciliosum* subsp. *borisii*: hairy, pale green, rounded rosettes and greenish-yellow flowers. The mountain houseleek, *S. montanum*, has small resin-scented, hairy, dark green rosettes and reddish-purple flowers.

Sempervivum montanum

Silene
(Campions, catchflies)

The sea campion, *Silene maritima*, is a laxly tufted plant with fleshy, grey-green leaves that looks good in the rock garden or growing in a wall niche or rock crevice. Its white flowers, which have characteristic, inflated calyces, appear in late spring and continue throughout summer. 'Flore Pleno' has double flowers.

Size H: 10–20cm/4–8in; S: 10–40cm/4–16in. **Aspect** Sun or part-shade. **Hardiness** Fully hardy. **Soil** Any, well-drained.

Other species *S. acaulis*: moss campion, quite different from the sea campion, forms moss-like, bright green cushions that are studded with small, solitary, pink flowers throughout summer.

Tropaeolum polyphyllum

Soldanella
(Alpine bells)

Dainty, tufted alpines with leathery, kidney-shaped leaves and slender stalks carrying one or several pendent, fringed bells in spring. The mountain tassel, *S. montana*, forms small mounds that bear lavender-blue flowers; subsp. *hungarica* is the easiest form to grow in the garden.
Size H and S: 5–15cm/2–6in. **Aspect** Sun or part-shade. **Hardiness** Fully hardy. **Soil** Moist, acid.
Other species *S. villosa*: creeping underground stolons and hairy stems with deeply fringed bells; needs peaty soil in part-shade.

Sowbreads see *Cyclamen*

Speedwells see *Veronica*

Stonecrops see *Sedum*

Stork's bills see *Erodium*

Symphyandra

A genus of biennials or short-lived perennials with attractive, pendent, bell-shaped flowers. *S. hoffmannii*, a biennial, often seeds around and bears pyramidal panicles of creamy-white flowers from mid-summer to early autumn.
Size H: 15–20cm/6–8in; S: 10–20cm/4–8in. **Aspect** Sun or part-shade. **Hardiness** Fully hardy. **Soil** Gritty, well-drained, alkaline to neutral.
Other species *S. wanneri*: more compact with purple-blue flowers.

Thrifts see *Armeria*

Tropaeolum polyphyllum

A tuberous plant with prostrate or trailing stems with numerous, hand-shaped, blue-grey leaves. The small, spurred, nasturtium-like flowers are deep yellow, appearing in early and mid-summer. This is a choice plant, but one that will spread widely in ideal conditions.
Size H: 5–10cm/2–4in; S: 20–50cm/8–20in. **Aspect** Sun. **Hardiness** Fully hardy. **Soil** Well-drained, gritty or loamy.

Veronica
(Speedwells)

V. prostrata forms dense mats with narrow, oval leaves and spikes of blue flowers from late autumn through to mid-summer. Some good cultivars include: 'Kapitan', bright blue; 'Spode Blue', china-blue; 'Trehane', deep violet-blue.

Size H: 10–30cm/4–12in; S: 20–50cm/8–20in. **Aspect** Sun. **Hardiness** Fully hardy. **Soil** Any, well-drained, loamy.

Viola
(Pansies, violets)

A large group of annuals and perennials, some of which seed around too freely for scree and rock gardens. *V. cornuta* forms lax mats with erect flowering stems. The fragrant, violet to lilac or white flowers appear constantly from late spring until early autumn.
Size H: 5–12cm/2–4¾in; S: 10–30cm/4–12in. **Aspect** Sun. **Hardiness** Fully hardy. **Soil** Any, well-drained.
Other species *V. calcarata*: long-spurred, pansy-like flowers in lilac, purple or white. *V. cenisia*: spreading runners and small, pansy-like flowers of violet. *V. lutea*: mountain pansy, spreading clumps with yellow, violet, white or bicoloured flowers.

Vitaliana primuliflora
syn. *Douglasia vitaliana*

A small, matted or somewhat cushion-forming evergreen with narrow, elliptical, grey-green leaves and numerous bright yellow, jasmine-like flowers in mid- to late spring.
Size H: 2–4cm/¾–1½in; S: 6–20cm/2¼–8in. **Aspect** Sun. **Hardiness** Fully hardy. **Soil** Well-drained, gritty, neutral to alkaline.

Whitlow grasses see *Draba*

Windflowers see *Anemone*

Small shrubs

Azaleas see *Rhododendron*

Brooms see *Cytisus, Genista*

Candytufts see *Iberis*

___

Clematis alpina

Although it is a woody climber, the alpine clematis can be extremely attractive in the rock garden if allowed to clamber through small shrubs or to drape itself over a large rock. It has paired, neatly lobed leaves and its pendent blue flowers with prominent white centres are followed by fluffy seedheads.
Size H: 2–3m/6–10ft; S: 1–2m/3–6ft. **Aspect** Shade or part-shade. **Hardiness** Fully hardy. **Soil** Moist, well-drained.

___

Cytisus
(Brooms)

A large genus of deciduous or semi-evergreen shrubs, only the smaller of which are suitable for the rock garden. *C. ardoinii*, is a dwarf, hummocky shrub with arching stems and small, trifoliate leaves that are downy when young. It has masses of golden pea-flowers in mid- and late spring. 'Cottage' is the best dwarf form.
Size H: 8–12cm/3–4¾in; S: 10–20cm/4–8in. **Aspect** Sunny. **Hardiness** Fully hardy. **Soil** Well-drained, alkaline.
Other species *C. × beanii*: neat, dwarf, up to 40cm (16in) high, with sprays of golden flowers. *C. decumbens*: prostrate with wiry stems and bright yellow flowers.

Daphne

One of the loveliest groups of shrubs for the alpine garden, daphnes can be evergreen or deciduous. Their often scented, four-lobed, tubular flowers are borne in spring. Plants greatly resent disturbance once established.

Deciduous species: *D. mezereum* bears small clusters of reddish-purple or pink flowers on leafless, erect branches as late winter slips into early spring. These are followed in mid-summer by shiny, scarlet berries.
Size H: 30–60cm/1–2ft; S: 20–50cm/8–20in. **Aspect** Sun or part-shade. **Hardiness** Fully hardy. **Soil** Leafy loam, neutral to alkaline.

Evergreen species: *D. petraea* 'Grandiflora', a compact shrub with glossy, elliptical leaves, is excellent in troughs. Large, bright pink flowers are borne from mid to late spring.
Size H and S: 20–50cm/8–20in. **Aspect** Sun. **Hardiness** Fully hardy. **Soil** Well-drained loam.
Other species *D. arbuscula*: very slow-growing, eventually forming mounds 20cm (8in) high, with tough, leathery, shiny leaves and deep pink flowers in mid-spring to early summer; excellent for troughs and raised beds. *D. cneorum* 'Eximia': spreading mounds 90cm (3ft) across, with slender stems, narrow, oblong leaves and deep rose-pink flowers in mid- to late spring.

___

Dryas
(Mountain avens)

These carpet-forming, evergreen subshrubs bear attractive eight-

Daphne mezereum

There is a pleasing range of colourful and shapely small shrubs ideally suited to the alpine garden. Slow-growing, they will remain in proportion to the rock garden, scree or trough in which they are planted.

petalled flowers that are followed by feathery fruits. *D. octopetala*, the most commonly seen species, has small, oak-like, dark green leaves that are woolly-white beneath. The white flowers are borne on spindly stalks from late spring to mid-summer. The cultivar 'Nana', a compact form, is the best choice for the smaller rock garden.
Size H: 4–8cm/1½–3in; S: 20–60cm/8in–2ft or more. **Aspect** Sun. **Hardiness** Fully hardy. **Soil** Well-drained, humus-rich, neutral or alkaline.

Erinacea anthyllis
(Hedgehog broom)

The slender, much-branched, greyish-green stems of this small, hummocky shrub are covered in spines and the small trefoil leaves are rather insignificant. The blue-violet pea-flowers are borne in clusters in late spring and early summer. It dislikes disturbance. **Size** H and S: 10–30cm/4–12in. **Aspect** Sun, sheltered. **Hardiness** Fully hardy when mature. **Soil** Well-drained, gritty, alkaline.

Iberis sempervirens

Genista
(Brooms)

A genus of often spiny, deciduous shrubs with characteristically yellow pea-flowers. *G. lydia* is a non-spiny shrub with arching green stems that are covered in bright yellow flowers in late spring and early summer. **Size** H: 30–40cm/1–1½in; S: 30–60cm/1–2ft. **Aspect** Sun. **Hardiness** Fully hardy. **Soil** Well-drained, alkaline to neutral.

Other species *G. delphinensis*: prostrate with bright yellow flowers from late spring to mid-summer.

Hedgehog broom
see *Erinacea anthyllis*

Helianthemum nummularium
(Rock roses)

An easy and colourful dwarf evergreen shrub with slender, spreading stems radiating from a central stock. Bright yellow flowers are borne in terminal racemes in summer. There are many cultivars available in a wide range of colours. **Size** H: 15–25cm/6–10in; S: 20–25cm/8–10in. **Aspect** Sun. **Hardiness** Fully hardy. **Soil** Well-drained, alkaline to neutral.

Hypericum
(St John's worts)

Some of the smaller shrubby members of this genus are good floriferous rock garden plants with paired leaves and showy yellow flowers with numerous stamens. Subshrubby *H. olympicum* has erect, woody-based stems and oval, greyish leaves. Its large, lemon-yellow flowers, arranged in terminal clusters, appear from the end of spring until mid-summer. 'Citrinum' has cream to pale yellow flowers.

Size H: 15–30cm/6–12in; S: 10–40cm/4–16in. **Aspect** Sun. **Hardiness** Fully hardy. **Soil** Well-drained.

Iberis
(Candytufts)

The shrubby species in this group make excellent rock garden subjects and provide good spring flower colour. Their four-petalled flowers are borne in rather flat clusters, with the outer petals characteristically larger than the inner ones. *I. sempervirens* forms spreading mounds of leathery, deep green leaves which bear white flowers in mid- and late spring. **Size** H: 15–30cm/6–12in; S: 30–60cm/1–2ft. **Aspect** Sun. **Hardiness** Fully hardy. **Soil** Well-drained.

Lithodora diffusa
syn. *Lithospermum diffusum*

A rather bristly evergreen shrub with intricate branches and narrow, deep green leaves. The salver-shaped flowers are a striking gentian-blue and are borne in late spring and early summer. 'Grace Ward' has deep blue flowers while those of 'Heavenly Blue' are pale blue and smaller. **Size** H: 20–30cm/8–12in. S: 30–60cm/1–2ft. **Aspect** Sun. **Hardiness** Hardy except in very exposed positions. **Soil** Acid or neutral.

Marjorams see *Origanum*

Mountain avens see *Dryas*

Mulleins see *Verbascum*

Origanum

(Marjorams)

Small, aromatic shrubs, much loved by bees and butterflies, with simple, paired leaves. *O. rotundifolium* is a spreading, deciduous plant with thin, woody stems and oval leaves. The tubular, two-lipped, pale pink flowers are borne in nodding heads surrounded by conspicuous, yellow-green bracts. **Size** H: 15–25cm/6–10in; S: 15–30cm/ 6–12in. **Aspect** Sun. **Hardiness** Fully hardy. **Soil** Well-drained, gritty.

Other species *O. amanum*: deciduous, rarely more than 15cm (6in) high, with heart-shaped, pale green leaves and long-tubed, bright pink flowers; frost-hardy; the form *album* is white.

Rhododendron

(Rhododendrons, azaleas)

Ranging from large trees to small prostrate shrubs, the acid-loving plants in this huge and popular group are noted for their brazen displays of bright blooms, but only the smallest are suitable for alpine gardens and of those only a few can be listed here. The alpenrose, *R. ferrugineum*, is an ever-green shrub with elliptical, deep green, rusty-backed leaves. The clusters of small, pink to crimson, trumpet-shaped flowers are borne from early to mid-summer. **Size** H and S: 30–60cm/1–2ft. **Aspect** Part-shade. **Hardiness** Fully hardy. **Soil** Moist, peaty, acid.

Other species *R. campylogynum*: variable, but one of the best with clusters of drooping, waxy bells ranging from rosy purple to deep pink or blackish-

purple. *R. camtschaticum*: deciduous with thin stems to 20cm (8in); bright green leaves and pink, salver-shaped flowers in late spring and early summer. *R. hirsutum*: similar to *R. ferrugineum* but with paler, bristle-margined leaves, green on the reverse, and the only rhododendron that will grow on alkaline soils. *R. impeditum*: low-growing evergreen with small clusters of mauve or purplish-blue flowers.

Rock roses
see *Helianthemum nummularium*

St John's worts see *Hypericum*

Salix

(Willows)

Willows, a large genus of deciduous trees and shrubs, bear male and female catkins on separate plants. Generally easy to cultivate, only the small alpine species are suitable for the rock garden. *S. reticulata* is a prostrate species with shiny, oval leaves that are netted with veins above and are silky-white with hair beneath. The long-stalked catkins stand erect above the leaves in early and mid-summer. **Size** H: 4–8cm/1½–3in; S: 8–30cm/ 3–12in. **Aspect** Sun or part-shade. **Hardiness** Fully hardy. **Soil** Cool, moist, humus-rich.

Other species *S. retusa*: mat-forming with small, oval leaves notched at the apex and small, yellow catkins. *S.* × 'Boydii': very slow-growing, small, gnarled-looking bush with small, rounded, grey leaves, to 60cm (2ft) high after many years.

Verbascum

(Mulleins)

V. dumulosum is an evergreen subshrub that forms a broad mat of elliptical, grey-green leaves. In late spring and early summer it produces numerous, short, bright yellow racemes of five-petalled flowers. **Size** H: 10–25cm/4–10in; S: 20–50cm/8–20in. **Aspect** Sun, sheltered. **Hardiness** Frost-hardy, dislikes winter wet. **Soil** Well-drained, gritty. **Other species** *V.* 'Letitia': rather spiky, evergreen, hummocky hybrid with paler yellow flowers with reddish-orange centres produced continuously from late spring to mid-autumn.

Willows see *Salix*

Rhododendron impeditum

Crevice plants

Plants which grow in rock crevices and the cracks in walls, whether stone or brick, provide valuable additional interest in the alpine garden. Some of these plants have already been described in the section on Perennials which starts on page 106.

Lewisia cotyledon

Acantholimon glumaceum
Resembling a hedgehog, this spiny, evergreen plant forms rounded hummocks of stiff, deep green leaves. The short spikes of star-shaped, pink flowers appear in early and mid-summer.
Size H: 6–12cm/2¼–4¾in; S: 10–20cm/4–8in. **Aspect** Full sun. **Hardiness** Fully hardy. **Soil** Well-drained, neutral to alkaline.

Alyssum saxatile see page 106

Antirrhinum
(Snapdragons)
Often freely seeding but short-lived, this attractive, primarily Spanish genus bears small, distinctive flowers, often on rather brittle stems. *A. molle* makes a many-branched, somewhat sprawling plant with soft, rounded leaves and white or pale pink flowers with a yellow 'mouth'.
Size H and S: 10–30cm/4–12in. **Aspect** Sun or part-shade. **Hardiness** Frost-hardy. **Soil** Any, well-drained, neutral to alkaline.

Arabis caucasica
see page 107

Aubrieta deltoidea
see page 107

Campanula portenschlagiana
see page 107

Chiastophyllum oppositifolium
see page 108

Corydalis lutea see page 108

Erigeron karvinskianus
(Wall daisy)
A semi-evergreen perennial with a mass of thin stems and small, lance-shaped leaves. The small, daisy-like flowers open white, with a central disk of yellow stamens, but gradually turn pink then purple. Often seeds freely.
Size H: 10–20cm/4–8in; S: 10–30cm/4–12in. **Aspect** Sun or part-shade. **Hardiness** Fully hardy. **Soil** Any, well-drained.

Erinus alpinus see page 109

Erodium petraeum see page 109

Globularia cordifolia
Covered with tiny, leathery, deep green, oval leaves, this mat-forming, creeping evergreen perennial has rather woody stems. The small, globose, blue or lavender-blue flowerheads are borne on short stalks from late spring to mid-summer.
Size H: 3–5cm/1¼–2in; S: 10–20cm/4–8in. **Aspect** Full sun. **Hardiness** Fully hardy. **Soil** Well-drained, neutral to alkaline.

Golden drops see *Onosma*

Haberlea
H. ferdinandi-coburgii is a tufted, evergreen perennial of one to several deep green rosettes made up of elliptical,

leathery, toothed leaves that are hairy underneath. The elegant sprays of white-throated, lilac or violet-blue, tubular flowers are borne in clusters on a common stalk from late spring through to early summer.
Size H: 10–15cm/4–6in; S: 10–40cm/4–16in. **Aspect** Shade or part-shade. **Hardiness** Fully hardy. **Soil** Moist, peaty or loamy.
Other species *H. rhodopensis*: very similar, but with soft hairs on both surfaces; 'Virginalis', white.

Horminum pyrenaicum
see page 110

Lewisia
Semi-succulent, rosetted plants with flashy flowers. *L. cotyledon* has large, evergreen rosettes of leathery, oblong, toothed leaves. The flowers range in colour from white to pink and purple, being red, orange and yellow in some strains. They are borne in clusters on long stalks from late spring to mid-summer. Cotyledon Hybrids are available in shades of pink and purple, and the Sunset Strain has flowers in a range of bright colours, particularly orange, red, apricot and yellow.
Size H: 10–25cm/4–10in; S: 8–20cm/3–8in. **Aspect** Part-shade. **Hardiness** Fully hardy but dislikes excess winter wet. **Soil** Well-drained, gritty.

Onosma
(Golden drops)
O. echioides forms bristly clumps with rather woody lower stems and numer-

ous narrow, untoothed leaves. The drooping, tubular, yellow flowers are borne in clusters at the stem tips throughout the summer.
Size H and S: 15–30cm/6–12in. **Aspect** Full sun. **Hardiness** Fully hardy, except in very exposed conditions. **Soil** Well-drained, neutral to alkaline.
Other species *O. alborosea*: more vigorous with white flowers that slowly change to pink, from late spring to mid-summer.

Penstemon newberryi
see page 111

Polemonium pulcherrimum
A tufted, bright green perennial with numerous pinnate leaves. The small, bell-shaped, bluish-purple flowers with pale yellow centres are borne on lax sprays throughout summer.
Size H: 20–40cm/8–16in; S: 15–30cm/6–12in. **Aspect** Sun or part-shade. **Hardiness** Fully hardy. **Soil** Any, well-drained, neutral to alkaline.

Ramonda
Highly attractive plants with rather flat rosettes of rough, toothed leaves. The african violet-like flowers are borne in small clusters on a common stalk. *R. myconi* (syn. *R. pyrenaica*), the most common species in alpine gardens, has flat flowers of blue, mauve or pink and, rarely, white in late spring and early summer.
Size H: 6–10cm/2¼–4in; S: 8–15cm/

Ramonda myconi

3–6in. **Aspect** Shady. **Hardiness** Fully hardy. **Soil** Moist, peaty or loamy.
Other species *R. nathaliae*: very similar to *R. myconi* but with lavender or lilac flowers.

Saponaria ocymoides
see page 114

Saxifraga cochlearis, S. longifolia, S. paniculata, S. 'Southside Seedling', *S.* 'Tumbling Waters'
see pages 114–15

Sedum acre, S. spathulifolium
see page 115

Silene maritima 'Flore Pleno'
see page 115

Snapdragons see *Antirrhinum*

Wall daisy
see *Erigeron karvinskianus*

Dwarf conifers

Only very slow-growing and truly dwarf conifers, which will not outgrow their allotted space in just a few years, are suitable for the alpine garden. A small selection of some of the best is presented here. They all share the same requirements: **Aspect** Sun. **Hardiness** Fully hardy but some may scorch in exposed, very windy sites. **Soil** Any, well-drained.

Abies
(Firs)

A. balsamea 'Nana' is very slow-growing, forming a compact, rounded,

Abies balsamea 'Nana'

deep green bush that bears attractive buds in winter.
Size H: 10–30cm/4–12in; S: 10–50cm/10–20in.
A. concolor 'Glauca Compacta' (syn. *A. concolor* Compacta'), a dwarf form of the colorado white fir, makes an irregular, rounded shape. Its steely blue colour is especially prominent in early summer.
Size H: 20–120cm/8in–4ft; S: 20cm–1.5m/8in–5ft.

Cedrus
(Cedars)

C. deodara 'Golden Horizon' is a graceful, semi-prostrate, golden form of the deodar cedar, the branches having weeping tips.
Size H: 20–75cm/8in–2½ft; S: 30–120cm/1–4ft.

Chamaecyparis
(Cypresses)

C. lawsoniana 'Aurea Densa' makes a dense dome of bright golden foliage year round, but is particularly effective during winter.
Size H and S: 10–50cm/4–20in.
C. lawsoniana 'Ellwood's Pillar' forms a narrow column of rather feathery, blue-grey foliage.
Size H: 20–90cm/8in–3ft; S: 5–30cm/2–12in.
C. lawsoniana 'Gnome' forms a rather irregular dome of deep green.
Size H and S: 50cm/20in.
C. lawsoniana 'Green Globe' makes a dense, neat globe of bright green foliage.
Size H and S: 5–30cm/2–12in.

C. obtusa 'Nana Pyramidalis' makes a dense, deep green, cone shape with a pronounced leading shoot.
Size H: 20–60cm/8in–2ft; S: 30–60cm/1–2ft.
C. pisifera 'Filifera Nana' grows as a compact dome with whip-like branches.
Size H and S: 20–60cm/8in–2ft.
C. pisifera 'Nana' makes a very slow-growing, dense, blue-green bun.
Size H: 5–20cm/2–8in; S: 5–30cm/2–12in.

Cypresses see *Chamaecyparis*

Firs see *Abies*

Juniperus
(Junipers)

J. communis 'Blue Pygmy' is a very dwarf, slightly irregular bun with steel-blue foliage.
Size H and S: 5–15cm/2–6in.
J. communis 'Compressa', perhaps the best of all for the alpine garden, makes a dense, pointed column of grey-green.
Size H: 20–75cm/8in–2½ft; S: 5–20cm/2–8in.
J. procumbens 'Nana' is a mat-forming plant with bright green foliage that is good for banks.
Size H: 10–20cm/4–8in; S: 20–75cm/8in–2½ft or more.
J. squamata 'Blue Star', one of the finest of all small conifers, forms a dense, rounded bush with bright bluish foliage.
Size H: 20–50cm/8–20in; S: 20–60cm/8in–2ft.

Picea

(Spruces)

Picea abies 'Ohlendorfii' is rounded at first, becoming columnar. Deep green and very neat, it resembles a dwarf Christmas tree.

Size H and S: 20–90cm/8in–3ft.

P. abies 'Reflexa' is a prostrate, deep green plant with irregular shoots. It can be tied to a stake to form a dwarf weeping shape.

Size H: 10–30cm/4–12in; S: 4m/13ft if left unchecked.

P. glauca var. *albertiana* 'Conica' (syn. *P. glauca* 'Albertiana Conica') is a widely grown conifer that forms a neat pyramidal or conical shape. In spring its young shoots are a bright yellow-green.

Size H: 30cm–1.5m/1–5ft or more; S: 30–120cm/1–4ft.

P. glauca var. *albertiana* 'Echiniformis' is a dwarf, flat-topped, deep green bun.

Size H: 10–50cm/4–20in; S: 20–90cm/8in–3ft.

P. omorika 'Nana' is a rounded to egg-shaped plant. The deep green foliage has a white reverse.

Size H and S: 20–90cm/8in–3ft.

P. pungens 'Globosa', a dwarf form of the colorado blue spruce, forms a broad, rounded shape with a short leader. Its silver-blue colour is especially intense during spring and early summer.

Pinus

(Pines)

P. heldreichii subsp. *leucodermis* 'Compact Gem' is a dense dwarf conifer which forms a broad conical or rounded shape, with shiny, dark green foliage. It is slow-growing, gaining on average only 2.5cm (1in) a year.

Size H and S: 10–50cm/4–20in.

P. heldreichii subsp. *leucodermis* 'Schmidtii' is a fine dwarf plant, forming an egg-shaped dome with shiny, dark green foliage.

Size H and S: 10–30cm/4–12in.

P. mugo 'Humpy' is a dwarf and compact form of the mountain pine. It makes a rounded bush with deep green foliage and has prominent buds in winter.

Size H: 10–40cm/4–16in; S: 10–50cm/4–20in.

P. strobus 'Reinshaus' is an excellent compact, rounded, deep green dwarf pine.

Size H and S: 10–60cm/4in–2ft.

P. sylvestris 'Doone Valley', a dwarf scot's pine, forming a rather irregular, deep green cone shape.

Size H and S: 20–90cm/8in–3ft.

P. sylvestris 'Nana' makes a dense, somewhat irregular, egg-shaped mound of deep green.

Size H and S: 10–50cm/4–20in.

Red cedars see *Thuja*

Spruces see *Picea*

Taxus

(Yews)

Taxus baccata 'Dwarf White', a compact form of the common yew, has a spreading habit. Its foliage is deep green but the needle-leaves are edged with white.

Size H and S: 10–75cm/4in–2½ft.

Picea pungens 'Globosa'

Dwarf conifers are a valuable adjunct to the alpine garden, providing year-round interest but especially during the dull winter months. They are also important in the design of the rock garden as special features or as accents among the rocks.

Thuja

(Red cedars)

T. orientalis 'Aurea Nana' is very slow-growing, making a neat and compact, beautifully egg-shaped bush. Its foliage is golden during the summer, turning bronze and green during the winter.

Size H and S: 10–60cm/4in–2ft.

Yews see *Taxus*

Index

Page numbers in *italics* refer to illustrations; numbers in **bold** to the chapter on Key Plants.

Abies see Firs
Acaena microphylla 65
Acantholimon glumaceum 43, *46*, 52, *54*, 73, *76*, **120**
Achillea
  A. ageratifolia 16, *98*
  A. tomentosa 65
Acid beds 57–63
Acid soils 18
Acid-loving plants 18, 36, *43*
Adiantum pedatum see Maidenhair fern
Aethionema 46, **106**
  A. grandiflorum see Persian stone cress
  A. pulchellum 106
Ajuga see Bugle
Alchemilla mollis see Lady's mantle
Alkaline soils 18
Allium see Ornamental onions
Alpenrose *(Rhododendron ferrugineum)* 119
Alpine bells *(Soldanella)* 11, **116**
  S. hungarica 116
  S. montana 116
  S. villosa 116
Alpine catchfly *(Lychnis alpina)* **111**
Alpine garden, types of 22–3
Alpine Garden Society 9
Alpine house 23, 87–97
  displaying plants 90–1
  heating 93
  suitable plants 95, 97
Alpine lawns 23, 64–7
  construction 64
  feature plants 65, *66–7*
Alpine poppy *(Papaver alpinum)* 21, *54–5*, 56, 111
Alpine thrift *(Armeria juniperifolia)* 46, *54–5*, 107
Alpine toadflax *(Linaria alpina)* 56
Alyssum **106**
  A. montanum 52, *54*
  A. saxatile 43, *45*, 46, *66*, 72, 106
Anagallis tenella 53, *53*
Anchusa caespitosa 85, *85*
Androsace see Rock jasmines

Anemone see Windflowers
Antennaria dioica see Cat's foot
Anthemis 11
  A. montana 54, *54*, 75
Anthyllis montana 50–1, 65
Antirrhinum see Snapdragons
Aquilegia see Columbines
Arabis see Rock cresses
Arenaria balearica 77
Armeria see Thrifts
Asarum europaeum 62
Asperula suberosa 74, **107**
Asplenium trichomanes see Maidenhair spleenwort
Astilbe chinensis var. *pumila* 50–1
Aubrieta 17, *72*, 101, *101*, **107**
  A. deltoidea 43, 107
Autumn 103
Azaleas *(Rhododendron)* **119**

Balloon flowers *(Platycodon grandiflorus)* **112**, *112*
Bark chippings 57
Basal cuttings 30, *30*
Bellflowers *(Campanula)* 11, *21*, **107**
  C. aucheri 21
  C. carpatica 21, *31*, 107
  C. cochleariifolia see Fairy's thimble
  C. portenschlagiana 54, *55*, 75, 107
  C. zoysii 85, *94*
Berberis × *stenophylla* 42
Betula nana 62
Bird damage 26, *27*
Bistorts *(Polygonum)* 9, **112**
  P. affine 112
Bloodroot *(Sanguinaria)* 60
Blue poppies *(Meconopsis)* **111**
  M. cambrica see Welsh poppy
  M. horridula 21, *58*, 111
  M. quintuplinervia 111
Bog primulas *(Primula)* 48
Bonemeal 28, 45, 101
Brooms *(Cytisus)* **117**
  C. ardoinii 117
  C. × *beanii* 117
  C. decumbens 117
Brooms *(Genista)* **118**
  G. delphinensis *54–5*, 56, 118
  G. lydia *19*, 42, *50–1*, 56, *66*, 118

Bugle *(Ajuga)*, propagation 103
Bulb frames 23, 97
  suitable plants 97
Bulbs 21, 23
  dead-heading 101
  peat beds 60
  rock gardens 44–5, *45*
Buttercups *(Ranunculus)* 11

Calcareous chippings 28
Caltha palustris see Marsh marigold
Campanula see Bellflowers
Campions *(Silene)* **115**
Candytufts *(Iberis)* **118**
  I. sempervirens 47, 118, *118*
Carlina acaulis see Carline thistle
Carline thistle *(Carlina acaulis)* 55, 102
Cassiope 62, *80*
Catchflies *(Silene)* **115**
Cat's foot *(Antennaria dioica)* 64
Cedars *(Cedrus)* **122**
  C. deodara 122
Cedrus see Cedars
Celmisia **108**
  C. coriacea 62, 108
Ceterach officinarum see Rustyback fern
Chamaecyparis see Cypresses
Chamaemelum nobile 64, *66*
Chiastophyllum oppositifolium *46*, **108**
Chionodoxa gigantea 101
Chrysanthemopsis hosmariense (syn. *Leucanthemum hosmariense)* **108**
Cistus see Sun roses
Clay soils 34
Clematis alpina **117**
Cloches 26, *26*
Clover *(Trifolium pratense)* 12
Cobweb houseleek *(Sempervivum arachnoideum)* *20*, **115**
Cold frames 26, 94
Colours, winter 100
Columbines *(Aquilegia)* 25, **106–7**
  A. alpina 50–1
  A. flabellata 106–7
Compost
  container alpines 78–9

peat beds 59
  propagation 29, 30
  raised beds 71
  rock gardens 35–6
Conifers
  see also Dwarf conifers
  planting 42
Contained alpines 69–87
Containers
  alpines 78–82
  feature plants 78, *80–1*
Convolvulus cneorum 36
Corydalis **108**
  C. flexuosa 60, *62*, 108
  C. lutea 74, *77*, 108
  C. solida 44, 108
Cowslip *(Primula veris)* 57
Cranesbills *(Geranium)* 11, **110**
  G. cinereum 21, *99*, 110
  G. dalmaticum 110
Creeping bluet *(Hedyotis michauxii)* **110**
Crevice plants **120–1**
  dry stone walls 73, 74
  rock gardens 39, 40, *40*, *43*
  rocky coast *13*
  tufa 84–5, *84*
Crocuses *(Crocus)* 11, *96*
  C. goulimyi 44
Cushion alpines 20
  potting 89
Cuttings, propagation 29–31
Cyclamen see Sowbreads
Cymbalaria
  C. muralis 77
  C. pallida 74
Cypresses *(Chamaecyparis)* **122**
  C. lawsoniana 122
  C. obtusa 122
  C. pisifera 122
Cytisus see Brooms

Dactylorhiza
  D. elata 50–1
  D. maculata see Marsh orchids
Daphne 27, **117**
  D. arbuscula 81, *81*, 117
  D. cneorum 42, *46*, 117
  D. kamtschatica var. *jezoensis* 100
  D. mezereum 100, 117, *117*
  D. petraea 'Grandiflora' 117
Devil's claw *(Physoplexis comosa)* 26, 85, *85*, 95, **112**

Dianthus see Pinks
Dionysia 20, 92
  D. bryoides 89
  D. tapetodes 8, *8*
Dividing plants 31, *31*
Dodecatheon see Shooting stars
Double potting *89*, 90
Douglasia vitaliana see *Vitaliana primuliflora*
Draba see Whitlow grasses
Dragonmouth *(Horminum pyrenaicum)* 110
Drainage, rock gardens 34, 41
Dryas octopetala see Mountain avens
Dry walls 22–3, 72–3, *76–7*
Dwarf bulbs, rock garden 44–5
Dwarf conifers *13*, *17*, 100, **122–3**
Dwarf plants, rock gardens 42–3
Dwarf rowan *(Sorbus reducta)* 42, *47*, 103
Dwarf shrubs 20, 43, 78

Edelweiss *(Leontopodium alpinum)* 43, *54–5*, **110**
Edraianthus graminifolius 52, *54–5*
Epimedium 35, 57, 60
Epipactis gigantea 62
Eranthis hyemalis 44
Erigeron karvinskianus see Wall daisy
Erinacea anthyllis see Hedgehog broom
Erinus alpinus see Fairy foxglove
Erodium see Stork's bills
Erythronium 60, *62*
Euphorbia myrsinites 47
Euryops acraeus 47, *99*
Evening primroses *(Oenothera)*
  O. caespitosa 111
  O. missouriensis 102, 111, *111*

Fairy foxglove *(Erinus alpinus)* *16*, 69, *109*, **109**
  dry stone wall *76*
  early summer *98–9*
  rock garden *46*
  scree garden 56
Fairy's thimble *(Campanula cochleariifolia)* *46*, 52, *76*, 107

Fascination of alpines 7–13
Feeding 28
  spring 101
Felicia amelloides 36
Ferns
  container alpines 82
  peat beds 59, 60, *62–3*
  shady troughs 80
Fertilizers 28
  bulbs 45
  spring 101
Fescue grasses (*Festuca*) 18,
  66, *66*
Firs (*Abies*) **122**
  A. balsamea 122, *122*
  A. concolor 122
Flat sites, rock gardens 41
Flaxes (*Linum*) *54–5*, **111**
  L. arboreum 111
  L. perenne 47
  L. suffruticosum 75, 111
Frames 23, 94, 97
French lavender (*Lavandula*
  stoechas) 36
Fritillaries (*Fritillaria*) *93*
  F. aurea 87
  F. meleagris see Snakeshead
  fritillary
Frost protection 93
Fungal control 96

Galanthus see Snowdrops
Gaultheria trichophylla 103
Genista see Brooms
Gentiana see Gentians
Gentians (*Gentiana*) 11, **109**
  autumn 103
  G. acaulis (syn. *G. kochiana*)
  43, 45, 47, 66, 74, 109
  G. depressa 8, *8*
  G. × macaulayi 103
  G. ornata 24
  G. septemfida 21, 109
  G. sino-ornata 58, *62*, 103,
  109
  G. × stevenagensis 103
  G. ternifolia 80
  G. verna 52, *54–5*, 101
  spring 101
Geranium see Cranesbills
Glass environment 88
Globularia
  G. cordifolia **120**
  G. nudicaulis 42, *42*
  G. repens 74, 81, *81*

Golden drops (*Onosma*) **121**
  O. alborosea 69, 121
  O. echioides 121
Grape hyacinths (*Muscari*) 44
Grasses, alpine lawn 64
Growing conditions 18–19
Gunnera magellanica 50
Gypsophila **110**
  G. aretioides 52, *54–5*, 85
  G. repens 12, 21, *54–5*, 110

Haberlea 88, **120–1**
  H. ferdinandi-coburgii 120–1
  H. rhodopensis 77, *80*, 121
Habitats 9–11
Hacquetia epipactis *62–3*, 110,
  110
Hardiness 18–19, 93
Hardwood cuttings 30, *30*
Hawk weed (*Hieracium*) *9*
Hedgehog broom (*Erinacea*
  anthyllis) *54–5*, 56, **118**
Hedyotis michauxii (syn.
  Houstonia caerulea) see
  Creeping bluet
Helianthemum see Rock roses
Herbaceous perennials 21
Hieracium see Hawk weed
Horminum pyrenaicum see
  Dragonmouth
Horned violet (*Viola cornuta*)
  10–13, 29, 47, *55*, 116
Hortag 91
Hosta 19, 48, 57
  H. sieboldiana 50–1
Houseleeks (*Sempervivum*) 22,
  52, *79*, **115**
  S. arachnoideum see Cobweb
  houseleek
  S. ciliosum subsp. *borisii* 115
  S. montanum see Mountain
  houseleek
Houstonia caerulea see
  Creeping bluet
Hypericum see St John's worts
Hypertufa 78, *79*

Iberis see Candytufts
Incarvillea mairei 21, **110**
Irises (*Iris*) 19
  dwarf bearded *99*
  I. cristata 63, 77, 80
  I. histrioides 100
  I. pumila 47
  I. reticulata 100

  I. sanguinea 50, *50*
  poolside plants 48
Irishman's cuttings 30, *30*
Island rock gardens 41, *41*

Jeffersonia dubia 63
Junipers (*Juniperus*) **122**
  J. communis 47, 56, 75, 81,
  81, 122
  J. procumbens 122
  J. squamata 122
Juniperus see Junipers

Key plants
  background 106
  crevices **120–1**
  dwarf conifers **122–3**
  perennials **106–16**
  small shrubs **117–19**

Labelling 25, 44, 102
Lady's mantle (*Alchemilla mollis*)
  50–1, *57*
Lavender (*Lavandula*) 13
  L. stoechas see French
  lavender
  summer 102
Leaf cuttings 30, *30*
Leafmould 57
Leontopodium alpinum see
  Edelweiss
Leucanthemum hosmariense
  see *Chrysanthemopsis*
Lewisia 88, **121**
  L. cotyledon 76, 82, *120*, 121
  L. tweedyi 91, *92*
Lichens, winter 100
Lilies (*Lilium*)
  L. columbianum 10
  L. formosanum var. *pricei* 60,
  63
  L. regale 63
Lime in rock gardens 36
Limestones, rock gardens 36–7
Linaria alpina see Alpine toadflax
Linnaea borealis 63
Linum see Flaxes
Lithodora diffusa (syn.
  Lithospermum diffusum) **118**
Lithospermum diffusum see
  Lithodora diffusa
Liverworts 28
Lobelia pedunculata see *Pratia*
Lychnis alpina see Alpine
  catchfly

Maidenhair fern (*Adiantum*
  pedatum) 60, *62*, 80
Maidenhair spleenwort
  (*Asplenium trichomanes*) 77,
  80
Maintenance
  alpine garden 26–8
  alpine houses 94–6
  alpine lawn 64
  autumn 103
  peat beds 61
  spring 101
  summer 102
  winter 100
Malcolmia 11
Marjorams (*Origanum*) 102,
  119
  O. amanum 119
  O. rotundifolium 119
Marsh marigold (*Caltha*
  palustris) 50, *50–1*
Marsh orchids (*Dactylorhiza*
  maculata) *9*, 48
Mat-forming plants, alpine lawns
  65
Matted alpines 20–1
Matteucia struthiopteris 63
Meconopsis see Blue poppies
Merry bells (*Uvularia grandiflora*)
  63
Mesembryanthemum 36
Milkworts (*Polygala*) **112**
  P. calcarea 112
Morisia monanthos *54–5*
Moss campion (*Silene acaulis*)
  115
Mosses, removal 28
Mountain avens (*Dryas*
  octopetala) 64, 74, **117**
Mountain houseleek
  (*Sempervivum montanum*)
  115, *115*
  alpine lawn *67*
  dry stone wall *76*
  rock garden *47*
  scree garden *55*
Mountain pansy (*Viola lutea*) 11,
  116
Mountain pride (*Penstemon*
  newberryi) 47, 69, 76, 111
Mulleins (*Verbascum*) **119**
  V. dumulosum 119
Muscari see Grape hyacinths
Muscari azureum see
  Pseudomuscari

Narcissi (*Narcissus*) 45, *93*
  N. asturiensis 101
  N. cyclamineus 44, 60, *63*
  N. poeticus see Poet's
  narcissus
Netting 26, *27*

Obtaining plants 24
Oenothera see Evening primrose
Onion see Ornamental onion
Onosma see Golden drops
Orchids, peat beds 60
Origanum see Marjorams
Ornamental onions (*Allium*) 44
  A. flavum 102
  A. senescens 102
Outcrops, building 38, *38*
Oxalis 81
  O. adenophylla 45, 47, 70, 75
  O. purpurea 97

Pansies see Violas
Papaver see Poppies
Paraquilegia anemonoides 26, *85*
Pasque flowers (*Pulsatilla*) 11,
  21, 27, **114**
  P. alba 114
  P. alpina 28
  P. alpina subsp. *apiifolia* 7, 28
  P. halleri 114
  P. occidentalis 8, *8*
  P. rubra 47, 67, 114, *114*
  P. vernalis 55, *55*
  P. vulgaris 67, 114
  spring 101
Peat beds 23, 57–63
  construction 57–9, *58*
  feature plants 59–60
Penstemon **111**
  P. newberryi see Mountain
  pride
  summer 102
Perennials
  key plants **106–16**
  weeds 27
Pernettya 103
Persian stone cress
  (*Aethionema grandiflorum*) 54,
  54, 106
Phlox 16, **112**
  P. adsurgens 112
  P. divaricata 63
  P. douglasii 112
  P. subulata 35, *55*, 112
  summer 102

Physoplexis comosa (syn.
    Phyteuma comosum) see
    Devil's claw
Picea see Spruces
Pines (*Pinus*) **123**
    P. heldreichii subsp.
    leucodermis 123
    P. mugo 123
    P. strobus 123
    P. sylvestris 123
Pinks (*Dianthus*) 25, **108–9**
    D. alpinus 54–5, 75, 80, *81*,
    108
    D. deltoides 74, 109
    D. erinaceus 43, *46*, 52, 54,
    54–5, 109
    D. petraeus 109
    raised bed *72*
    summer *99*, 102
Pinus see Pines
Plant sources 24
Planting
    alpine garden 22–3, 24–5
    alpine houses 89, *89*
    alpine lawns 65–7, *66–7*
    autumn 103
    bulbs 97
    containers 82
    crevices 40, *41*
    peat beds 60–1
    poolsides 48
    raised beds 74–5
    rock gardens 42–4
    screes 52
    spring 101
    summer 102
    tufa 84–5
    wall crevices 73–4
Platycodon grandiflorus see
    Balloon flowers
Plunge beds 90–1, *91*
Poet's narcissus (*Narcissus
    poeticus*) 9, *9*
Polemonium pulcherrimum **121**
Polygala see Milkworts
Polygonum see Bistorts
Pools
    construction 49, *49*
    liners 48
    rock gardens 41, 48–50
Poppies (*Papaver*) **111**
    P. alpinum see Alpine poppy
    P. miyabeanum 111
Potentilla
    P. aurea 65

P. cuneata 66, *67*, 74
Pots, alpine house 88–90, *89*
Pratia pedunculata (syn. *Lobelia
    pedunculata*) 47, *67*, 77, 80,
    112–13
Primroses (*Primula*) 11, **113**
    P. allionii 87
    P. auricula 113
    P. bhutanica 113
    P. bulleyana 113
    P. frondosa 113
    P. gracilipes 63
    P. hirsuta 40
    P. japonica 57, 113
    P. marginata 74, 101, 113
    P. petiolaris 113
    P. polyneura 113
    P. prolifera 48, *50–1*, 113
    P. pulverulenta *50–1*, 113
    P. rosea *50–1*, 113
    P. sieboldii 113, *113*
    P. sikkimensis 113
    P. veris see Cowslip
    P. vulgaris 63, 101, *101*, 113
    P. whitei 63
    propagation 103
Primula see Primroses
Propagation 29–31
    autumn 103
    potting 88–90, *89*
    spring 101
    summer 102
    winter 100
Protecting plants
    seedlings 101
    winter 26, *26*, 100
Pseudomuscari azureum (syn.
    Muscari azureum) 101
Pterocephalus perennis (syn. *P.
    parnassii*) 21, *54–5*, *67*, **114**
Pulsatilla see Pasque flowers
Pygmy foxglove (*Erinus alpinus*)
    16

Rainfall 18
Raised beds 22, 70–3, *71*
    construction 72–3, *72*
    materials 71
    preparation *73*
Ramonda 21, 88, **121–2**
    R. myconi 8, *8*, *39*, 77, 80,
    121, *121*
    R. nathaliae 85, 121–2
    R. pyrenaica see *R. myconi*
Ranunculus glacialis 10

Red cedars (*Thuja*) **123**
    T. orientalis 123
Red spider mites 96
Rhododendrons (*Rhododendron*)
    119
    R. campylogynum 119
    R. camtschaticum 119
    R. cinnabarinum 63
    R. 'Curlew' 63
    R. ferrugineum see Alpenrose
    R. hirsutum 119
    R. impeditum 119, *119*
    R. williamsianum 63
Rhodohypoxis baurii 45, 75, *81*
Rock cresses (*Arabis*) **107**
    A. × *arendsii* 'Rosabella' 107
    A. caucasica 43, 107
    spring 101
Rock gardens 22
    creation 34–40, *34*
    pools 48–50
Rock jasmines (*Androsace*)
    106
    A. ciliata 84
    A. hirtella 81, 85, *85*
    A. lanuginosa 52, 106
    A. sarmentosa *46*, 52, 106,
    107
    A. sempervivoides 54
    A. vandellii 40
    potting 89
Rock roses (*Helianthemum*) 11,
    66–7, *72*, 102
    H. nummularium **118**
Rock soapwort (*Saponaria
    ocymoides*) 12, *76*, **114**
Rocks
    movement of 37, *37*
    placement 39
    rock gardens 36–7
    scree beds 52
Root cuttings *30*, 31
Rosette cuttings 30, *30*
Rosetted alpines 21
Routine maintenance see
    Maintenance
Rowan see Dwarf rowan
Rustyback fern (*Ceterach
    officinarum*) *76*, 85

Sagina subulata 64, 66, *67*, 84
St John's worts (*Hypericum*)
    118
    H. olympicum *14–15*, *36*, 118
Salix see Willows

Sand beds 88, 91
Sanguinaria see Bloodroot
Santolina 36
Saponaria ocymoides see Rock
    soapwort
Saxifraga see Saxifrages
Saxifrages (*Saxifraga*) 18, **114**
    alpine house 87
    containers 79, 82
    hybrids 114–15
    rock garden 47
    S. burseriana 75, *85*, 114, 115
    S. cochlearis 43, *81*, 114
    S. cotyledon 114
    S. cymbalaria 21
    S. fortunei 63
    S. 'Gregor Mendel' (syn.
    S. × *apiculata*) 100, 115
    S. grisebachii 74, 114
    S. hypostoma 20
    S. longifolia 76, 114
    S. oppositifolia 43, 75, 114
    S. paniculata 81, 114
    S. retusa 85, *85*
    S. 'Tumbling Waters' *50*, 67
    spring 101
    tufa *83*, 85
    winter 100
Scilla bifolia 44
Scottish Rock Garden Club 9
Scree beds 22, *22*, 52–3
    construction 53, *53*
Scree gardens 54–6, 100
    feature plants *54–6*
Scutellaria see Skullcaps
Sea campion (*Silene maritima*)
    115
Seasons 100–3
Sedum see Stonecrops
Seedlings, pest protection 101
Seed, sowing 29, *29*
Semi-ripe cuttings 30, *30*
Sempervivum see Houseleeks
Shade
    alpine house 92, *92*, 101
    containers 80, *80*, 82
    summer 102
Shooting stars (*Dodecatheon*)
    D. meadia 49
    D. pulchellum 49, *62*
Shortia soldanelloides 63
Shrubs 117–19
    peat beds 60
Silene **115**
    see also Campions; Catchflies

S. acaulis see Moss campion
S. maritima see Sea campion
Sinks, container alpines 78
Sisyrinchium 81
    S. bermudiana 47, 66, *67*
    S. brachypus 47
    S. douglasii 80
Siting
    alpine houses 88
    alpine lawns 64
    container alpines 78–9
    flat land 41
    islands 41, *41*
    peat beds 57
    raised beds 70
    rock gardens 34
Skullcaps (*Scutellaria*)
    S. alpina 43
    S. orientalis 66, *67*, 103
Slug baits 100
Snakeshead fritillary (*Fritillaria
    meleagris*) 101, *101*
Snapdragons (*Antirrhinum*) **120**
    A. molle 120
Snowdrops (*Galanthus*) 44
    G. regina-olgae 103
    winter 100
Softwood cuttings 30, *30*
Soils
    alkalinity 18
    growing conditions 18
    rock gardens 35
Soldanella see Alpine bells
Sorbus reducta see Dwarf
    rowan
Sowbreads (*Cyclamen*) **108**
    C. album 108
    C. cilicium 44, 103
    C. coum 44, *46*, 61, *62*, 100,
    108
    C. goulimyi 103
    C. graecum 92
    C. hederifolium 44, 103, 108,
    108
    C. intaminatum 45
    C. niveus 103
    C. purpurescens 62
    C. repandum 60, 103, 108
    C. rohlfsianum 92
Sowing 100
    procedures 29, *29*, 103
Speedwells (*Veronica*) **116**
    V. cinerea 43
    V. gentianoides 57
    V. prostrata 116

Spring 101

Spring-flowering hardy alpines 44

Spruces *(Picea)* **123**

  P. abies 123

  P. glauca var. *albertiana* 47, *56*, 123

  P. mariana 47

  P. omorika 123

  P. pungens 123, *123*

Stepping stones, alpine lawns 64, *65*

Sternbergia

  S. colchiciflora 45

  S. lutea 103

  S. sicula 103

Stone chippings 28

Stonecrops *(Sedum)* *42, 43,* **115**

  S. acre see Wall pepper

  S. cyaneum 115

  S. ochroleucum 115

  S. pulchellum 115

  S. spathulifolium *14–15,* 115

Stork's bills *(Erodium)* *14–15,* **109**

  E. petraeum 109

  E. reichardii (syn. *E. chamaedrioides)* 52, 109

Succulents, rock gardens *43*

Summer 102

Summer-flowering hardy alpines 44

Sun roses *(Cistus)* *13*

Sun-loving container alpines 78

Sunny troughs 81–2, *81*

Symphyandra **116**

  S. hoffmannii 116

  S. wanneri 116

Taxus see Yews

Temperature, hardiness 18–19

Terraced peat beds 58, *58*

Terracotta pots *79*

Thrifts *(Armeria)* *18,* **107**

  A. juniperifolia see Alpine thrift

  A. maritima *43, 66,* 107

  containers *82*

Thuja see Red cedars

Thymes *(Thymus)* *18*

  alpine lawns 65

  summer 102

  T. serpyllum *47, 64, 66, 67*

Top-dressing 28, 101

Tree line alpines 11

Trefoils *(Trifolium)* *11*

Uvularia grandiflora see Merry bells

Trifolium see Clover; Trefoils

Trillium

  T. grandiflorum *21, 63*

  T. rivale *63, 80*

  T. sessile see Wake-robin

Trollius

  T. europeaus 50

  T. pumilus 50

Tropaeolum polyphyllum *116,* **116**

Troughs 22

  container alpines 78, *80–1*

Tufa

  see also Hypertufa

  alpines 83–5

  dry stone walls 72

  rock gardens 37

  suitable plants 84–5, *85*

  use of 83

Tulipa see Tulips

Tulips *(Tulipa)* 93

  T. aucheriana 96

  T. batalinii 101

  T. linifolia 44, 75, *90,* 101

  T. tarda 75

Vaccinium vitis-idaea 63

Ventilation, alpine houses 88

Veratrum 10

Verbascum see Mulleins

Veronica see Speedwells

Vine weevil 96

Violas *(Viola) 82,* **116**

  alpine house *87*

  ·*V. calcarata* 116

  V. cazorlensis 85

  V. cenisia 116

  V. cornuta see Horned violet

  V. delphinantha 85

  V. lutea see Mountain pansy

Violets *see* Violas

Vitaliana primuliflora (syn. *Douglasia vitaliana)* **116**

Wake-robin *(Trillium sessile)* 63

Wall daisy *(Erigeron karvinskianus) 14–15, 36,* **120**

Wall pepper *(Sedum acre) 76,* 115

Walls 22–3, *69,* 73–4

Watering

  alpine houses 92–3, 95

  container plants 102

  summer 102

tufa plants 84

Weed control 25, 26–8

  rock gardens 34

  tufa 84

Welsh poppy *(Meconopsis cambrica) 35,* 111

Whitlow grasses *(Draba)* **109**

  D. aizoides 101, 109

  D. longisiliqua 26

  D. polytricha 85

Willows *(Salix)* 42, **119**

  S. lanata 47

  S. reticulata 119

  S. retusa 119

Windflowers *(Anemone)* **106**

  A. blanda *105,* 106

  A. magellanica *16, 102,* 106

  A. nemorosa see Wood anemone

  A. ranunculoides 62

Winter 26, 100

Wood anemone *(Anemone nemorosa)* 62

Wooden slats, alpine houses 92

Yellow alyssum *(Alyssum)* 106

Yews *(Taxus)* **123**

  T. baccata 123

Acknowledgments

Author's acknowledgments

I would like to thank my wife, Christine, for reading the original manuscript and for her invaluable comments.

Publisher's acknowledgments

The publisher would like to thank the following photographers and organizations for their kind permission to reproduce the photographs in this book:

1 Peter Murray; 2 Brigitte Thomas; 4–5 Jerry Harpur (Homelands, Balscote); 6–7 Hans Reinhard/Bruce Coleman; 8 top Michael D. Jones; 8 above Christopher Grey-Wilson; 8 centre Smith Stainton/Collections; 8 below Christopher Grey-Wilson; 9 Christopher Grey-Wilson; 10 above Tom Leach/Oxford Scientific Films; 10 below Christopher Grey-Wilson; 12 Christopher Grey-Wilson; 13 Michelle Lamontagne; 14 Neil Campbell-Sharp; 16 Christopher Grey-Wilson; 17 Brigitte Thomas; 18 Eric Crichton; 19 Jerry Harpur (designer: Christopher Grey-Wilson); 20 left Christopher Grey-Wilson; 20 right Marijke Heuff; 21 left Christopher Grey-Wilson; 21 right Michelle Lamontagne; 22 above Clive Nichols (Turn End Garden, Buckinghamshire); 22 below Christopher Grey-Wilson; 23 Brigitte Thomas; 24 Christopher Grey-Wilson; 25 Neil Campbell-Sharp (Mrs Royd's Alpine Garden, Wiltshire); 27 Marijke Heuff; 28 Christopher Grey-Wilson; 29 Photos Horticultural; 31 Michelle Lamontagne; 32–3 Eric Crichton; 34 Michelle Lamontagne; 35 above Hugh Palmer; 35 below Eric Crichton; 36 Brigitte Thomas; 37 Michelle Lamontagne; 38 Hugh Palmer; 39 Marijke Heuff; 40 left Christopher Grey-Wilson; 40 right Frithjof Skibbe/Oxford Scientific Films; 41 Brigitte Thomas; 42 left Michelle Lamontagne; 42 right Jerry Pavia/Garden Picture Library; 43 JS Sira/Garden Picture Library; 45 Christopher Grey-Wilson; 48 Peter Stiles; 49 Karl Dietrich-Bühler/Elizabeth Whiting & Associates; 52 left Christopher Grey-Wilson; 52 right John Glover; 53 Michelle Lamontagne; 56 Jerry Harpur (designer: Christopher Grey-Wilson); 57 JS Sira/Garden Picture Library; 58 Christopher Grey-Wilson; 59 Hugh Palmer; 60 left John Glover; 60 right Christopher Grey-Wilson; 61 Eric Crichton; 65 John Glover/Garden Picture Library; 68–9 Boys Syndication; 70 Neil Campbell-Sharp; 71–2 Hugh Palmer; 74 Neil Campbell-Sharp; 75 Michelle Lamontagne; 79 Neil Campbell-Sharp; 82 Eric Crichton; 83–5 Christopher Grey-Wilson; 86–7 Robert Rolfe; 88 Michelle Lamontagne; 89 John Glover; 90–1 Christopher Grey-Wilson; 92 Eric Crichton; 93 John Glover; 94 Andrew Lawson; 95 Photos Horticultural; 96 above Christopher Grey-Wilson; 96 below Photos Horticultural; 97 Christopher Grey-Wilson; 98–9 Christopher Grey-Wilson/Nature Photographers; 100 Elizabeth Whiting & Associates; 101 Christopher Grey-Wilson; 102 Christopher Grey-Wilson/Nature Photographers; 103 Christopher Grey-Wilson; 104–5 John Glover; 108 Christopher Grey-Wilson; 109 Neil Campbell-Sharp; 110 Photos Horticultural; 111 John Glover; 112 Photos Horticultural; 113 Michelle Lamontagne; 114 Neil Campbell-Sharp; 115 Vaughan Flemming/Garden Picture Library; 116–19 Photos Horticultural; 120 Michelle Lamontagne; 122 Photos Horticultural.

The publisher also thanks: Barbara Mellor, Jackie Matthews, Barbara Nash and Janet Smy.

Index compiled by Indexing Specialists, Hove, East Sussex BN3 2DJ.